MANAGED & CARE YOU:

THE CONSUMER GUIDE
TO MANAGING
YOUR HEALTH CARE

DISCLAIMER

MANAGED & CARE YOU:

THE CONSUMER GUIDE TO MANAGING YOUR HEALTH CARE

Michael E. Cafferky

McGraw-Hill, Inc.
New York St. Louis San Francisco Auckland Bogotá Caracas
Lisbon London Madrid Mexico Milan Montreal New Delhi Paris
San Juan Singapor Sydney Tokyo Toronto

MANAGED CARE & YOU: THE CONSUMER GUIDE TO
MANAGING YOUR HEALTH CARE

1 2 3 4 5 6 7 8 9 0 DOC DOC 95

ISBN 0-07-600759-6

This book was composed and set in Minion by Carol Woolverton
Studio.

To Lois and Gene

Table of Contents

PART I: The Managed Care System: Background and Structure

CHAPTER 1
What Is Managed Care and How Did It Become So Popular?   3

CHAPTER 2
Types of Managed Care Organizations   17

About the Author

A Certified Healthcare Executive through the American College of Healthcare Executives, Michael E. Cafferky has been in the healthcare industry since 1982. He is the administrator for integrated healthcare systems at Walla Walla General Hospital in Washington. He has worked in the past for Pacific Hospital of Long Beach, Kettering Medical Center, and National Medical Enterprises. In his current position he is responsible for managing a physician-hospital organization. He was an elected member of the Board of Directors for Healthcare Executives of Southern California and the secretary of that organization's Managed Care Planning Committee.

An experienced trainer and public speaker, Mr. Cafferky has given speeches and seminars in both the United States and Eastern Europe. As a consultant Mr. Cafferky has served dozens of organizations including for-profit corporations, non-profit organizations, and the U.S. Peace Corps.

Mr. Cafferky holds advanced degrees in both public health and marketing. He is the author of *Patients Build Your Practice: Word-of-Mouth Marketing for Healthcare Practitioners* and *Let Your Customers Do the Talking: 225+ Word-of-Mouth Marketing Tactics Guaranteed to Boost Profits.*

Preface

Managed Care and You is written from the premise that the more you know about managed care, the more your experience as a managed health care plan enrollee will be satisfying. If you are an informed managed care consumer, you will:

1. Have realistic expectations of what your experience will be like,
2. Be less surprised when you see the differences between managed care and traditional health insurance,
3. Be prepared for every step in the process of becoming and remaining a satisfied member or subscriber of a managed healthcare plan,
4. Know how to collaborate with your managed care team,
5. Be able to assist family members and friends who are enrolled in a managed care organization.

This book was written with several groups in mind including the following:

1. Members of managed care organizations who want to know more about how their health plan works,
2. People who are thinking about joining a managed care organization but want more information before making their choice,
3. Employees of companies that offer one or more managed care plans for employee's benefit,
4. Senior citizens who are faced with the choice of whether to remain under the traditional Medicare program or to enroll in an HMO for seniors.
5. State Medicaid beneficiaries who are being encouraged to enroll in HMOs,
6. Health benefits managers of companies and labor unions who are either considering offering an HMO to workers, measuring the quality of HMOs, or are counseling employees on the various health plan options available.

This is not a book on health care policy. It answers two important questions: "How does managed care work?" and "How can you practically make the best of it if you are a member of a managed care organization?" Assorted "how-to" books have been written on various single aspects of health care: choosing a health insurance plan, knowing the difference between one health plan and another, choosing a doctor, surviving a hospital experience, and being a wise health care consumer. *Managed Care & You* goes one step further by bringing all the pieces together in the context of today's managed care environment. You will find in these pages information not provided in other consumer publications.

Specifically, I show you

1. How to select a quality managed care organization, doctor, and hospital,
2. How managed care physicians work,
3. What goes on behind the scenes,
4. How to navigate around your managed care organization during the process of care,
5. How your managed care team works when you are well or ill,
6. How to prevent problems from arising,
7. How to solve problems that may arise,
8. How you can fulfill your responsibilities as a health plan member,
9. How quality is measured and improved in managed care,
10. How you can be prepared for the future of managed care.

Managed care has many expressions across the country. In some regions it is far advanced compared with that found elsewhere. To the degree that I have represented the common elements of managed care found in most regions and most health plans I am gratified. Where I have come up short in describing the differences in managed care comparing one region or one health plan with another, I plead the limitations of time to research all the subtle differences, the space to write it all, and the patience of readers who have their own limitations in reading about the subject.

Managed care is here to stay. As a consumer advocate and a member of an HMO myself, I say why not know all you can about the organization to which you have entrusted the maintenance of that most precious of gifts, your personal health.

Michael E. Cafferky
Fontana, CA

Acknowledgments

I acknowledge the following individuals who graciously took the time to discuss managed care with me:

Clement Bezold, executive director of the Institute for Alternative Futures in Alexandria, Virginia.

Kathryn Clark, director of Service Quality Operations for Group Health Co-operative of Puget Sound in Seattle, Washington.

Russell Coile Jr., president of Health Forecasting Group in Santa Clarita, California.

Carol Cronin, vice president of *Health Pages Magazine,* in New York.

Ellen Eisner, director of Member Service for Harvard Community Health Plan in Brookline, Massachusetts.

Sam Ervin, CEO of SCAN Health Plan in Long Beach, California.

John Gabel, director of research, Group Health Association of America, the HMO industry trade association, in Washington, D.C.

Mary Gardiner-Jones, president of Consumer Interest Research Institute in Washington, DC.

Richard Hart, M.D. D.PH., dean of the School of Public Health at Loma Linda University, Loma Linda, California.

Mary Hodges, R.N., director of Utilization Management and Case Management of Universal Care Health Plan in Signal Hill, California.

Karen Ignagni, executive director of the Group Health Association of America in Washington, DC.

Pamela Kalen, executive director of Managed Health Care Association in Washington, DC.

John Ludden, M.D., medical director of the Harvard Community Health Plan in Brookline, Massachusetts.

Doug McKell, president of Physician Strategies 2000 in Franklin, Ohio.

Margaret O'Kane, executive director of the National Committee for Quality Assurance in Washington, DC.

William Osheroff, M.D., medical director of Pacificare Health System in Cypress, California.

Bill Petersen, M.D., medical director of the Health Outcomes Institute in Bloomington, Minnesota.

Jane Preston, M.D., president of the American Telemedicine Association in Austin, Texas.

John Renner, M.D., president of Consumer Health Information Research Institute in Independence, Missouri.

Alyce Sease, R.N., care coordinator at Kaiser Permanente of Southern California in Fontana, California.

Dr. Cary Sennett, director of clinical planning and improvement at Group Health Cooperative of Puget Sound in Seattle, Washington.

David Siegel, M.D., M.PH, medical director of Health Alliance Plan based in Detroit, Michican.

Jacque J. Sokolov, M.D., CEO of Advanced Health Plans, Inc. in Los Angeles, California.

Glen Spielman, director of Health Services for Geisinger Health Plan in Danville, Pennsylvania.

Charles Steller, executive director of the American Managed Care & Review Association in Washington, DC.

Sean Sullivan, president & CEO of the National Business Coalition on Health in Washington, DC.

Al Truscott, M.D., medical director of Group Health Cooperative of Puget Sound in Seattle, Washington.

Jim Walworth, president of Health Alliance Plan and executive vice president of the Henry Ford Health System in Detroit, Michigan.

Michael Weinstein, president of Managed Care Planning Associates in Encino, California.

Frederick J. Wenzel, president of the Medical Group Management Association in Engelwood, Colorado.

W. C. "Bill" Williams III, M.D., president of the National Association of Managed Care Physicians in Glen Allen, Virginia.

Bartley Yee, D.O., medical director of the Family Practice Clinic at Pacific Hospital in Long Beach, California.

Mark Zitter, president of The Zitter Group and the Center for Outcomes Information in San Francisco, California.

Joe Zupec, vice president of Health Plan Management Services in Atlanta, Georgia.

The Managed Care System: Background and Structure

What Is Managed Care and How Did It Become So Popular?

I recently joined a managed care organization, sometimes referred to as a *managed care network,* or simply as an MCO, because I need health services. This organization is known as a *health maintenance organization,* or HMO.

Managed care is not new to me, though, because I have worked in the health care industry for over twelve years watching managed care from behind the scenes. I have served on management committees, negotiated contracts between health plans and health care providers, read confidential reports and memos, and listened to insiders who really know how managed care works. But now I can see from an HMO member's point of view what this popular concept is all about.

As you might expect, any dedicated top-level manager who works for an HMO will assure you that becoming a member of a managed care organization is a smart move. However, what do the industry experts—those at the front lines of providing the care—say when confiding their true feelings about managed care? Whether you are one of the 50 million HMO members in the United States, one of the 70 million members of other types of managed care organizations, someone who is thinking about joining one of these health plans, or even if you already work in the health care field, this book offers you the view from the inside.

WHAT IS MANAGED CARE?

Until recently medical care was a system that provided care for you while other organizations or a third party arranged for the payment for those services. *Managed care* is a system that integrates the efficient delivery of your medical care with payment for the care. In other words, managed care includes both the financing *and* delivery of care. A list of the key management principles used by managed care organizations is shown in Figure 1-1.

Managed care organizations attempt to establish formal, contractual relationships with physicians and hospitals. These health plans attempt to squeeze the cost of care by wise *authorization procedures* and payment for services (see Chapter 8). They establish explicit standards to use in managing the use of health services, recruiting of physicians and nurses, and monitoring the financial health of the company.

Managed care organizations also use formal *utilization management* programs (see Chapters 10 through 13). Utilization management is a system that monitors the appropriateness of care before, during, and after the care is actually provided to you. Utilization management also includes a system to obtain authorization to use certain health services. In some organizations it includes medical supervision, continuing care planning, and discharge planning.

Bartley Yee, D.O., director of the Family Practice Residency program at Pacific Hospital of Long Beach, says that managed care "places a lot of emphasis on giving responsibility back to the patient to make decisions for their own health care. It also places a lot of emphasis on the physician being a good advocate for the patient, providing the patient with options and with information and helping to direct the health care."

When viewed on a patient-by-patient basis the cost savings by participating in managed care are relatively small. However, if the cost savings are multiplied across a large population of HMO members, the numbers increase noticeably. For example, employers can achieve cost savings in commercial HMO products,

1. Strong emphasis on primary care physicians
2. Utilization management tools such as
   a. Medical supervision
   b. Authorization systems
   c. Utilization review
   d. Case management
   e. Medical practice guidelines
   f. Continuing care planning
3. Quality monitoring and improvement
4. Decreased emphasis on hospital care
5. Interest in disease prevention and health promotion
6. Collaboration with you and your family
7. Selective contracting with physicians and hospitals
8. Emphasis on appropriate self care

FIGURE 1-1   Key principles of managed care.

and Medicare beneficiaries can, in some locations, achieve cost savings compared with fee-for-service Medicare.

Managed care includes the whole spectrum of care needed from birth to death, not just a few medical conditions. All types of health care organizations are included in managed care activities. Those concerned with cost savings, improving acessibility to patients, and standardizing treatment patterns for patients with similar conditions are often interested in managed care.

Managed care is an interactive process, says Joe Zupec, vice president of Health Plan Management, Inc., based in Atlanta. In the traditional world of insurance, he says, you filled out forms and the insurance company paid its portion of the bill. Under managed care you, your physician, and the health plan interact to determine the most appropriate care. Zupec sees managed care as more of a partnership between the physician, the health plan member, and the health plan. Managed care is a service that you *participate in* rather than just a place to send your claims for payment.

THE ORIGINS OF MANAGED CARE

America is now in its sixth phase of managed care. While many Americans for the first time are becoming aware of the terms "managed care" and "HMOs," the industry that got it started is moving with the energy of a rocket.

Phase One

Born over a hundred years ago out of necessity to care for workers with no source of care other than self care, prepaid medical groups began managed care's phase of infancy. The concept was simple: In exchange for a monthly fee, a few physicians agreed to provide medical services to a defined population of workers. Prepaid meant that the physicians received payment for services before the services were provided.

Then, in 1929 the Ross-Loos Health Plan was organized by two physicians who broadened the scope of prepaid health care to serve more than one employer. In this early phase, the terms "health maintenance organization" and "managed care organization" were not used.

For employers who purchased such a service, the main issue was access to care for their employees. Employees working in isolated areas couldn't ride into town to visit the physician whenever they needed. So, instead of the workers going to the physician, the physician in the prepaid medical group came to them.

In these early years, not all physicians liked the idea of prepaid medicine. Physicians in private practice jealously guarded their independence. A few were militantly against the early concepts of managed care, believing that prepaid medicine would take away the physician's autonomy.

Phase Two

Between the 1940s and 1960s managed care's second phase came and went. During this time the prepaid medical groups demonstrated that not only could they *provide* high quality care, but they could *manage* the care as well. Independent researchers found that the health of employees covered by the prepaid medical plans was as good or better than that of employees covered under popular insurance programs.

Phase Three

Managed care's race for public acceptance entered its third phase—that of official recognition—early in the 1970s when the U.S. Congress passed the Health Maintenance Organization Act of 1973. Under this Act, certain employers offering health care coverage as a benefit must offer at least one form of traditional insurance and at least one federally funded HMO. In addition, the government had the authority to assist federally qualified HMOs in getting off the ground by providing grants and loans.

Despite this assistance, in the decade that followed the managed care industry grew slowly. Three influences contributed to this slow growth. First, physicians in private practice staunchly resisted participating in HMOs. Without more physicians available, the health plans had a difficult time enrolling more new members. Second, HMOs were still learning how to be profitable. Some HMOs failed financially, sending waves of caution through the health care industry. Third, employer groups embraced traditional health insurance plans as the standard of health benefits.

Phase Four

By the mid 1980s, federal and state legislatures had tallied the votes. Policy makers placed an increasing emphasis on the financial strength of HMOs. During this decade HMOs demonstrated that a consistent application of a few central principles of managed care could keep workers healthy and reduce costs.

During the decade after the 1973 U.S. HMO Act, Medicare and Medicaid administrators experimented by applying the principles of managed care to their beneficiaries. Medicare is the federal hospital insurance system with supplementary medical insurance created for the aged (through the 1965 amendments to the Social Security Act). The totally disabled and blind are also eligible for benefits. Medicaid is a federally assisted, state-operated and -administered program that provides health care benefits to specified low-income persons. There are wide differences in coverage and benefits from state to state.

During this fourth phase other health plans began to try some of the management techniques that HMOs had developed. Some of these organizations included preferred provider organizations (PPOs) and the utilization review companies that began serving them, as well as traditional health insurance companies.

According to Joe Zupec, in the early days many employers offered an HMO plan on an experimental basis. But for those companies where managed care became popular with employees, this little experiment added on to traditional health insurance suddenly encompassed 40 percent of the health care business. Employers who had sweated over managing the costs of health care under traditional insurance began to realize that what they wanted to get out of traditional insurance was being transferred to managed care. It didn't take long to figure out that the train was going in the other direction. From then on getting the best value for their premium dollars became an obsession. It was during this period that the movement toward improving quality for managed health plans gained a foothold (see Chapter 19).

Phase Five

Managed care moved into its fifth phase in the late 1980s as HMOs began developing systems that actually improved the *managing* part of managed care. Several important components of managed care were developed, such as utilization review, case management, patient education, selective contracting with physician groups and hospitals, and the use of alternative venues for delivering care including surgery centers, home care services, and skilled nursing facilities.

Managed care was not without its critics. During the fifth phase critics held up for public ridicule the disadvantages and weaknesses of managed care organizations. The public reaction spurred the managed care organization administrators to begin making changes in the way health care was delivered.

Phase Six

By the early 1990s leaders in managed care organizations found the key to long-term success: maintaining a very close relationship between the health plans, the physicians, and hospitals. All three types of organizations realized that to improve patient satisfaction and further reduce operating costs they needed to share information and business objectives with each other, a process called integration.

For many years a few HMOs, like Kaiser Permanente, Group Health Cooperative of Puget Sound, and Family Health Plan (FHP), had been perfecting *integrated delivery systems.* These integrated systems usually involved a central ownership or control over the three largest players in health care services: the health plan, the physician group, and the hospital.

REENGINEERING THE SYSTEM

Market pressures for lower prices and higher quality are totally redesigning the industry. As the system is reengineered, enrollment will continue to grow rapidly (see Figure 1-2). Consequently, we are seeing the emergence of two themes. The first is *point-of-service* plans, an important consumer-oriented shift. Point of service is a way to expand the list of providers available to you whenever you need care (see Chapter 2). The second theme is the increased pace with which other health care insurance programs continue to mimic the managed care principles developed by HMOs.

Americans are still learning the how and why of managed care. During the next decade managed care organizations will be able to measure the actual health

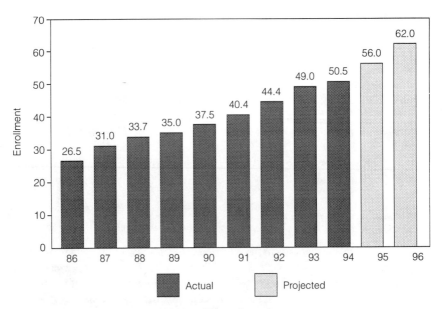

FIGURE 1-2   Growth trends in HMOs in millions of members.
Source: Used with permission of the SMG Marketing Group.

improvement of members. HMOs claim that they and their networks of health care providers are capable of producing the lowest-cost delivery of quality care in the nation. And the American employer community is now saying, "Don't just talk about it. Show it!"

In addition, the U.S. Department of Health and Human Services Agency for Health Care Policy and Research is developing a standardized consumer satisfaction questionnaire. John Gabel, Director of Research for the Group Health Association of America in Washington, D.C., reports that his association heads a group of 19 organizations that constitute an advisory committee to the Agency. Once developed and accepted for use by health plans, this questionnaire will generate information that consumers will be able to use to compare one plan with another.

THE STAKEHOLDERS OF MANAGED CARE

The growing strength of managed care affects every element of our nation's health care delivery:

- Hospitals have fewer patients. Patients who go to the hospital are more ill than patients in the past. Under managed care more patients are treated in settings other than the hospital. One result of this is that, on the average, patients who are in the hospital need a higher intensity of service than in earlier years. Consequently, the cost of care for each patient is going up as the reimbursement is going down.
- Physicians cannot afford to avoid participating in managed care even though the fees they receive may, in some cases, be lower than in the past.
- Traditional insurance companies that are not heavily involved in managed care see their enrollments eroding as managed care becomes stronger. Millions of people are still covered under traditional insurance programs that are now gearing up to become managed care organizations.
- Beneficiaries of government-sponsored health care (such as those signed up for Medicare and Medicaid) are being encouraged to join HMOs—and they are joining by the millions (see Chapter 4). Policy leaders are realizing that the momentum of the marketplace in the wider acceptance of managed care will create many of the changes in the health system that government desires.
- Employers, fed up with the high cost of care, are turning to managed care as the best current alternative to reduce their health care costs, improve quality of care, and enhance employee benefit packages.

■ Patients are learning new ways to relate with their physicians and hospitals. As one of the most important stakeholders in care, patients must be more involved in medical decision making.

Consumer confidence in managed care is growing. In five or six years the total number of HMO members may double what it is now. Currently HMO enrollment represents only about 19 percent of all insured people. By the year 2000 the proportion is likely to be 40 percent or higher.

YOUR MANAGED CARE TEAM

Under managed care, a team of managers of care share the responsibility for your health. This team is the central core group without which management is difficult, if not impossible, to achieve. It is composed of:

1. You. With your involvement in the management of your care, your care givers are better able to diagnose, treat, monitor, and advise you. If you are unable to make medical decisions for yourself, you should appoint a family member or guardian to participate in decision making.
2. Your *primary care physician,* sometimes referred to as a "PCP." This is the individual who watches over all aspects of the care process (see Chapter 3).
3. Your *primary nurse, nurse practitioner,* or *physician assistant.* Your primary care physician may bring the office nurse onto the management team to assist with day-to-day coordination, give you information referrals, and provide care for medical conditions that do not need a physician.
4. Your *utilization review coordinator.* A key advisor to you and your physician, this person constantly monitors the appropriateness of care (see Chapter 10).
5. Your *case manager.* This individual is responsible for coordinating the various levels of care that you may need. Sometimes your physician, a primary nurse, or a utilization review coordinator will fill the role of case manager (see Chapter 11).
6. Your *continuing care planner.* This person will assist you during the transition from the hospital to your home or to another facility that will continue to provide care for you. Sometimes the case manager fulfills the role of continuing care planner, and vice versa (see Chapter 13).
7. Your *medical* or *surgical specialist* (for example, a cardiologist or orthopedic surgeon). From time to time your management team will add other health care professionals to the team on a short-term basis. These physicians and

allied health professionals are specialists who give advice or perform specialized services.

8. Your health plan or medical group *medical director*. Your treatment team can go to the medical director if collectively they need extra advice. Even though you may never meet this person, he or she may be involved in the utilization review, case management, and coaching of the rest of the team.

REGIONAL VARIATIONS IN MANAGED CARE

Managed care is practiced differently in every corner of America, making it even more difficult to define. Employers and employees seem to have strong opinions about what they like and dislike about managed care programs. Joe Zupec says that in certain areas of the country people prefer the IPA model of HMOs (see Chapter 2). In other areas of the country people are happy with fully integrated systems of care, as provided by Kaiser Permanente or Group Health Cooperative of Puget Sound.

Even within the same region there are differences of opinion regarding the best way to practice managed care. This is one explanation for the many different forms of managed care organizations. Figure 1-3 lists some of these organizations.

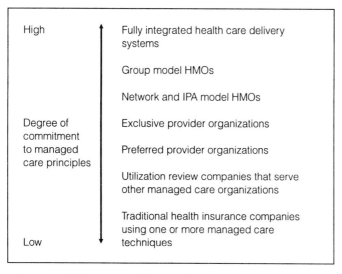

FIGURE 1-3 Different types of managed care organizations.

WHY MANAGED CARE IS SO POPULAR

Over 50 million people in America are members of HMOs, and another 70 million are assigned to PPOs. HMOs are in almost every state in the Union. Employers, government organizations, and the general population select HMOs and other managed care organizations for many reasons. Here are the most common ones:

1. Reduced health care costs. Those who purchase health care services are faced with rapid increases in health care costs. HMOs offer a way to control these costs by reducing inappropriate use of services, reducing or eliminating the duplication of care, and sharing financial responsibility with the employee.
2. HMO benefits are comparable to those of traditional insurance. According to Jacque Sokolov, M.D., CEO of Advanced Health Plans, Inc. in Los Angeles, California, the benefits of competing plans have become increasingly similar. The manner in which those benefits are delivered differentiates one health plan from another.
3. Accessibility. As managed care organizations mature, they are able to offer to enrollees physicians and hospitals that cover wide geographic regions. To compete with traditional insurance plans, managed care organizations must be able to deliver care to employees who live greater distances from the primary service area surrounding the employer's location.
4. Superior quality control methods. Managed care organizations now have methods to validate their quality of care. Many submit managed care practices carried out on behalf of their members to independent review (see Chapter 19).
5. High member satisfaction. Recent opinion polls show that Americans who are members of managed care organizations are as happy or happier with their health plans than their counterparts in other types of insurance plans. When satisfaction is high, members tend to recommend their health plan to others, influencing those who are deciding whether to join a managed care plan.
6. Satisfaction with managed care physicians. It is not always necessary to change physicians when joining a managed care plan. But if required to do so most members find that the new physician is as competent and caring as any physician that they have seen.
7. Coordination of care. In the fee-for-service market, the patient is often on his or her own when coordinating care. In managed care, physicians, nurses, and social workers take an active role in coordinating your care. In fact, says Dr. Bartley Yee, "the advocacy role that physicians take in some of the larger managed care organizations often results in assisting the patients

in gaining access to more services that they may not ordinarily receive in the fee-for-service environment. The larger managed care organizations attempt to make these services available to assist the physician in treating the health plan members."

8. Case management programs. The case manager assists you in navigating around the managed care organization. Members with particularly complex health problems find this service particularly helpful (see Chapter 11).

9. Availability of extra services. Health plans are adding services to help members navigate their way around the system. A few years ago, comments Dr. Yee, health plans were saying "How can we afford things like 24-hour telephone lines staffed with nurses?" Now they are saying, "We can't afford not to have them available."

MANAGED CARE IS NOT PERFECT

Some managed care organizations are going through growing pains, and some are simply better than others. Here are several of the problems managed care consumers have experienced over the years:

1. Limited choice of physicians. HMOs have been criticized for having fewer physicians and hospital providers from which health plan members may choose. In traditional health insurance you have the pick of almost any physician in the country. (This issue often makes more of a difference to those who see a physician on a regular basis or have to change physicians when joining the plan.) Health plan physicians counter this criticism by stating that seemingly unlimited choice is no choice if you don't know anything about the quality of the physician you are getting. During the last five years, however, HMOs have realized that to attract more members, they must first attract the best physicians available. In the cities where managed care has the highest penetration rates and the most competition, HMOs have signed up physicians who have the best reputations. Many managed care organizations conduct a thorough check of each physician's qualifications before letting that physician join the plan and then review that physician's credentials every two years.

2. Loss of control by physicians. Some patients and physicians have felt that managed care allows physicians less overall control of health care. Utilization management criteria and authorizations for care should be managed by the physicians who practice in your community. The trend in managed care is to let physicians in each local area to have the control.

3. Balancing cost and quality. Another problem is that some HMOs seem to be better at managing costs than managing care; in some cases this has been a valid criticism. HMOs are still learning and maturing in their ability to respond to consumer needs and to weigh these two competing demands.

4. Long waiting time for care. Some HMO members find that they wait longer to see their physicians or to receive special diagnostic procedures, opening up the question as to whether the quality of care is diminished. In any case, you should not have to wait longer than your doctor's non-HMO patients have to wait to receive services.

5. Shorter time with your physician. If the HMO or medical group gets so efficient that patients feel that they do not have adequate amount of time with their physicians, their strength in efficiency becomes a weakness.

6. Limited access to necessary services. Once in a while an HMO member may not receive the care that was expected. When this happens to many members or when the news media pick up a dramatic story, public perception of the HMO's quality can be harmed.

7. More rules to follow. In the traditional system of health care, if you got sick you went for care and your insurance paid for it. You may have had more paperwork to fill out, but you didn't have to wade through pages of instructions of what you could and could not do. It is true that managed care requires more consumer involvement in decision making than is required under traditional insurance. While some consumers consider this a disadvantage, others like to know more about what is going on.

8. Confusion about what is expected. More guidelines to follow can cause more confusion about what to do under certain circumstances, where to go and not go, and what is covered and not covered. Today many HMOs are investing time and money informing the public about how managed care works.

9. Insignificant cost savings. Employers with managed care organizations that do not have the best utilization management departments probably do not save as much money as those with well developed utilization management services. Also, in some cities the premiums for managed care organizations are roughly the same as for traditional health insurance. In addition, the premiums for HMOs in the most competitive markets are typically much lower than traditional health insurance products. Employers in these cities are demanding that managed care organizations make good on their promises for lower costs.

10. Inconvenient locations. This may or may not be true in your area, but for some people it has been an issue. This continues to be a problem for members who do not live or work close to the health plan facilities.

11. A perception that there is an additional layer of administrative work between the patient and the physician. The administration of managed care

organizations performs important services that you normally receive from traditional health insurance companies as well as additional services not available in other types of health plans.

You may be one of those people who have hesitated joining a managed care organization. If so, try to identify the reasons for your hesitation. Then—in addition to reading this book—talk to your family physician, a friend who is a member, or someone from an HMO, such as a medical director, to get a better perspective on the issue.

Types of Managed Care Organizations

You will find elements of managed care in almost all types of health plans. Health maintenance organizations (HMOs) have taken the lead in developing the management tools in managed care. However, *preferred provider organizations* (PPOs), *exclusive provider organizations* (EPOs), and other plans use managed care to some degree. Even traditional health insurance companies are copying some of the successful management approaches that HMOs pioneered.

Once a breed unto themselves, HMOs were clearly different from other forms of health plans. Now other types of health plans are incorporating managed care systems. Employers have demanded that other health plans offer the management benefits that HMOs offer. And HMOs are changing as well, since employers also have demanded that they develop the flexibility of traditional health plans, such as giving members more freedom to choose between physicians and hospitals.

Do not assume that one HMO has just one option to offer you. For example, if someone tells you that CIGNA Health Plan is a *staff model HMO,* this does not mean that CIGNA is *only* a staff model. A staff model health plan employs physicians on salary. CIGNA Health Plan may also have a group model in your region and in other regions. The *group model HMO* contracts with an independent group of physicians to provide services to health plan members. Another CIGNA plan may be an *independent practice association* (IPA) *model* under the same CIGNA name. The IPA model plan contracts with a collection of physicians who maintain their independent, private practices to treat other patients. Also, CIGNA may have a choice of several models or options to offer an employer.

Managed care plan options differ primarily along the following lines:

1. How many choices you have for physicians and hospital providers.
2. How much you pay out of your own pocket in copayments or deductibles.
3. How much control the health plan has over the types of health services you use. To you as a patient this may not seem all that important as long as you get good care from your physician.

TABLE 2-1

Types of Managed Care Organizations

	Choice of Provider	Control Over Use	Use of Managed Care Principles
Integrated delivery systems	moderate	high	high
Staff Model HMO	moderate	high	high
Group model HMO	low	high	high
Network model HMO	moderate	moderate	high
IPA model HMO	high	low	moderate
Direct contract model HMO	low	high	high
Point-of-service plans	high	low	moderate
EPO plans	low	moderate	moderate
PPO plans	high	low	low
UR company	moderate	moderate	moderate
Managed insurance	high	low	low

4. How much control the health plan has over its costs.
5. Location of providers. Some HMO options offer a high level of convenience by locating their physicians and ancillary services—such as X ray, medical laboratory, and physical therapy—in centralized locations. Other models have relationships with providers who are dispersed throughout the community.
6. How closely related the various providers are to each other and to the health plan. As you will see, providers of integrated delivery systems are closely affiliated and providers of traditional insurance plans are not. When a company owns or has a share of the ownership of all the providers, it usually has the ability to provide care at any level of need.

Table 2-1 summarizes the different types of managed care organizations. Although there are differences among these HMO options, they all have a legal responsibility to fulfill their obligations to you, to provide quality physicians and hospitals, and to offer the basic physician-patient relationship.

INTEGRATED DELIVERY SYSTEMS

Integrated delivery systems (IDS) are organizations that own most of the relevant companies needed to finance and deliver health care services to you. A computer network links every relevant provider of care, so that your managed care team has access to information about your health at the touch of a button. Jim Walworth, President of Health Alliance Plan in Detroit, Michigan, points out two advantages of fully integrated delivery systems over other forms of managed care:

> One is that there is a tendency to have greater continuity of care to the health plan member. There is a set of peer relationships among the physicians, nurses, and practitioners that is not found in the other models. There is also the uniqueness of the common medical record that stays with the individual regardless of who is providing the immediate next step of care. The other benefit is that within an integrated system you have much more control over instituting the process of improvement.

Currently there are very few completely integrated delivery systems. Staff model HMOs and group model HMOs usually come the closest to being fully integrated delivery systems. However, even these HMOs must contract with independent companies to provide what they cannot provide in certain geographic regions or for specific types of care.

STAFF MODEL HMOs

One of the earlier forms of HMOs, *staff model HMOs,* employ physicians who are salaried employees (staff) of the health plan. Staff model HMOs own their own clinics where their physicians are located.

Staff model HMOs hire physicians from the medical and surgical specialties that employees use most often. For specialty services that are used infrequently, the staff model may contract with one or more specialists who are in private practice in the community.

Staff model HMOs are noted for being skilled managers of medical services. Because the physicians are employees of the HMO, the health plan has a greater degree of control over what physicians do and don't do and what procedures are allowed and not allowed. They must meet the high standards of training and experience that other HMOs require. Although they are employees, physicians typically have a strong influence on the health plan's governing board of directors. In addition, staff model HMOs offer a high degree of one-stop shopping convenience with a variety of services at each of their clinics.

Because staff model HMOs hire their own physicians they may have higher expenses than other HMOs, so keeping operating costs under control is a challenge. To control costs staff model HMOs attempt to schedule patient visits efficiently. The challenge is to balance the patients' need to spend time with physicians with their need to have physicians be as productive as possible.

GROUP MODEL HMOs

In *group model HMOs,* the health plan contracts with an organized group of physicians called a medical group. Most medical groups who serve managed care plans are made up of many medical and surgical specialists. Because of this, these groups are sometimes referred to as *multispecialty medical groups.*

Under this relationship with the health plan, the physicians as a group contract to provide services for HMO members. Physicians in a multispecialty group are not employees of the HMO as in the staff model. Some physicians in the group may be salaried employees of the group and some physicians may be part owners. The physicians in multispecialty groups share facilities, computer systems, and support staff. Sometimes a health plan will contract exclusively with a group of physicians formed solely to serve members of that health plan. Other health plans contract with independent multispecialty medical groups to serve HMO members. These independent groups may serve members of more than one group model HMO as well as patients with other types of health insurance.

Through the medical group's own internal utilization management department, group model HMOs have strong controls over utilization—as in the staff model HMO—without having to maintain the high fixed costs of physician-employee salaries. Large multispecialty groups usually offer the one-stop shopping convenience that staff model clinics offer. Because the physicians in these groups treat a high proportion of HMO members compared with other types of patients, the physicians are well trained in managed care systems.

NETWORK MODEL HMOs

Network model HMOs try to overcome the shortcomings of the staff model and group model plans while preserving many of their advantages. In this model the health plan contracts with a network of medical groups spread out over a wide geographic region. These medical groups are independent and can be multispecialty or single specialty groups depending on the needs of the health plan in the area.

Network model HMOs typically have a larger list of physicians from which to choose. The network for the HMO may be totally different from one city to another. Network HMOs must spend more of their own resources for utilization management even if some of the groups with which they contract can fulfill this function.

IPA MODEL HMOs

In some locations of the country the *independent practice association* (IPA) *model* alone has given new HMOs the ability to compete with the more established managed care organizations.

An IPA is a group of physicians in private practice who sign contracts with the IPA for the purpose of providing care to HMO members. IPAs are owned either by a group of physicians or sometimes by a single physician.

To adequately serve the HMOs, independent practice associations must include under contract at least one physician from every medical and surgical specialty. These IPAs attempt to build large panels of primary care physicians to increase consumer choice, making them more attractive to both the health plan and the employer groups.

Some IPAs have less control than staff model or group model health plans over how medical services are used, although in some regions of the country, such as southern California, IPAs do have well-developed systems to monitor what services are used by health plan members.

IPAs that are managed by primary care physicians typically have more experience in controlling how health services are used than those managed by specialists. The problem of less control creates a challenge to the HMO: it may have to watch over how the physicians in the IPA use health services more closely than it would a medical group dedicated to the HMO.

IPAs give an HMO the ability to enter a new city and be operational within a few months at very little expense. The physicians in the IPA are free to care for members of any other type of health plan that will contract with them.

DIRECT CONTRACT MODEL HMOs

Most HMOs prefer to develop close working relationships with a few organizations that, in turn, can serve a wide region. For the past five years this has been the trend in cities where managed care is the most well developed. In some cases, however, HMOs choose to contract directly with physicians. This direct relationship with individual physicians has generated the *direct contract model HMO.*

Direct contract model HMOs attempt to increase the range of choices and geographic coverage for consumers. The trade-off is that the HMO has less control over how each individual physician uses health services. Since the physicians do not have an organized method of monitoring the use of services, the HMO must take this function entirely upon itself.

POINT-OF-SERVICE PLANS

Point-of-service (POS) *plans* allow health plan members to use any physician or hospital in the marketplace. In exchange for this increased freedom to choose providers, health plan members pay higher monthly premiums as well as higher copayments (see Chapter 18).

Consumer freedom to choose providers was the backbone of the traditional health insurance programs of the 1970s and 1980s. Before managed care became so popular, limitation on choice was one of the reasons why more employers did not offer HMOs to their employees. Now HMOs have brought back the freedom of choice and flexibility in the form of point of service. Currently POS is the fastest growing form of managed care plan.

Some POS programs are simply added to the managed care plans that already exist and employees can choose whether to sign up with the usual managed care plan or the POS plan. In other companies the employee can sign up for the POS plan but does not pay extra unless the point-of-service program is actually used. This is sometimes called a "dual option" program, meaning that the employee has two options at all times. For example, an employee can enroll in the dual option program but use the HMO physician most of the time. Whenever the employee decides to use a physician not signed up with the plan, he or she is accessing the second option. When this happens, the employee will probably pay a higher co-payment (see Chapter 18) for the physician's visit than would be paid if an HMO physician was used.

John Gabel reports that about 70 percent of HMOs now offer some kind of POS option. Even though there are merely 3.5 million HMO members currently enrolled in POS plans, about 90 percent of these never use the option. They simply want it available should they ever need to go outside the plan and use other physicians.

Figure 2-1 presents a summary of advantages and disadvantages of point-of-service plans.

Advantages
1. Increased choice of providers
2. Some degree of cost control
3. A measure of control over how health services are used
4. Increased savings when health plan network providers are used

Disadvantages
1. Increased complexity of the program means learning more about how to use the plan successfully
2. Increased risk of confusion over the details and mistakes in processing claims
3. Increased cost when providers outside of the health plan network are used

The bottom line: If the level of choice is not increased for you, point of service may not be your best option.

FIGURE 2-1   Advantages and disadvantages of point-of-service plans.

EXCLUSIVE PROVIDER ORGANIZATIONS

Another form of managed care organization is the *exclusive provider organization* (EPO). In the EPO model, used primarily in local markets for local businesses, the health plan contracts with a specific set of physicians and usually just one hospital to serve a specific employer. Health plan members who sign up with this program are required to receive health services from only the designated contracted exclusive providers unless they wish to pay for the total cost out of their own pocket. EPOs limit choice from among providers while preserving the benefits of the HMO managing how and what health services are used. If the point-of-service plan offers the greatest freedom of choice, the EPO probably offers the least freedom.

PREFERRED PROVIDER ORGANIZATIONS

During the late 1970s and early 1980s insurance companies attempted to control how and what health services were used by contracting with a selected group of physicians and hospitals. Because it cost too much for each insurance company to contract with individual physicians and hospitals in every area of the country, most insurance companies used an independent intermediary company, called the *preferred provider organization,* or PPO. A few larger insurance companies developed their own preferred provider organizations.

Preferred provider organizations establish and maintain a network of physicians and hospitals that are willing to provide care to insurance plan beneficiaries at a discounted fee. Some PPOs perform other functions for the insurance companies, such as monitoring how and what health services are used, evaluating claims for accuracy, and paying the claims. The range of services offered to the insurance company is different for each PPO.

As a consumer, you may be aware that you are signed up with a PPO and know which selected physicians are signed up as providers. Other than this your relationship with your health plan is very similar to that with traditional health insurance plans.

PPOs are very popular in America in spite of the growing popularity of HMOs. They usually offer wider choice of physicians in the community, but have much less control over how and what health services are used by beneficiaries. Unlike HMOs, however, PPOs are not responsible for both the financing and delivery of care.

UTILIZATION REVIEW COMPANIES

Utilization review companies are organizations that assist PPOs and traditional insurance companies in monitoring how and what health services are being used by health plan beneficiaries. Known simply as UR companies, they are not true managed care organizations since they are not responsible for either the financing or the delivery of care. They are responsible for traditional utilization review functions, such as authorization for services requested by the physician or the beneficiary, monitoring of and reporting on the medical necessity of services provided, and validating that claims submitted by either the patient or the provider have been authorized.

Roughly two-thirds of all workers who have health insurance are covered by their company's own health insurance plan. These companies are called "self insured" because they use their own money to pay for health services used by employees. Many of these self-insured companies contract with a utilization review organization to assist them in managing costs.

MANAGED INSURANCE

Traditional health insurance companies are also using some of the managed care principles. In the traditional health insurance plan the beneficiary simply submits claims for payment and the insurance company pays the bills. Some insurance plans use the services of a utilization review company or a PPO to help them manage the costs of care.

WHAT MODEL IS BEST FOR YOU?

You may have little choice of which model is offered to you. However, regardless of what models are available in your area, you should be able to assess your own health care needs. Use Figure 2-2 to evaluate your current health plan or the health plan you are thinking of joining.

1. What health plan model are you a member of (or thinking of becoming a member of)?
2. Does that health plan have more than one model for delivering health care? If so, what are the options?
3. Does the health plan offer the degree of choice that you need?
4. Is the physician's office convenient for you?
5. How many locations are there to serve you, both for physicians and for hospitals?
6. Is it important to you whether your physician is a salaried employee of the health plan, a member of a medical group, or in private practice? Why?
7. Does the health plan offer a computer communication system that assists it in providing high quality service any time of the day or night and anywhere you are in the country?

If you are considering a POS:
a. How wide a geographic region does the point of service cover?
b. If the network of providers is still under development (meaning that not all physicians and hospitals have signed up yet), what percent of the area is complete?
c. Are providers located near where you live or work?
d. Is there an adequate choice of providers available?
e. Does the point-of-service option increase choice for you?

You may want to refer to Chapter 5 for more information on how to evaluate a health plan.

FIGURE 2-2 Evaluate your health plan.

CHAPTER 3

Physicians within the Managed Care System

Ask the leading HMOs how they describe the ideal primary care physician and this is what you will hear: This physician is someone who:

1. Gives personal care
2. Is accessible to patients
3. Has a commitment to continuity of care rather than episodic care
4. Is skilled in coordinating the managed care team's effort
5. Educates the patient
6. Emphasizes health promotion and disease prevention

How does your physician compare with these qualities?

HMOs know that their reputations are built on the reputations of the primary care physicians. If new members have a positive experience with the primary care physicians, the word spreads. It is no wonder that HMOs are rivetted on the quality of primary care physicians. But this is only one reason why managed care plans are interested in primary care. Here is the rest of the story.

WHO ARE THE PRIMARY CARE PHYSICIANS?

Primary caregivers usually include the following types of physicians:

1. General practitioners. These physicians treat a variety of common illnesses. While not board certified in family practice, they are licensed. Board certification is a status awarded by a professional association indicating that the physician has met specific standards of knowledge and clinical skill within a specific field. Certification involves the passing of a written and oral ex-

amination administered by the professional certification committee. Some have completed residency training and were, at one point, board eligible. Others became general practitioners before board certification in family practice was available.

2. Family practitioners. These physicians are board certified in the specialty of family practice. They are trained to diagnose and treat a variety of common illnesses. Family practitioners treat people of all ages, including children and senior citizens.

3. Internal medicine physicians. Sometimes called internists (not to be confused with "interns" who are physicians in hospital training), these physicians are board certified or board eligible in the specialty of internal medicine. They are trained to diagnose and treat a variety of common and serious adult illnesses involving the body's major organ systems. Some internists get extra training and become subspecialists in areas such as cardiology, pulmonary medicine, and gastroenterology.

4. Pediatricians. Sometimes called "baby doctors," these physicians are board certified in pediatric medicine. Their training is similar to that of internal medicine specialists except that they are trained to diagnose and treat illnesses in children from birth to 18 years of age.

5. Obstetricians and gynecologists. These physicians are board certified in the medical and surgical skills needed to diagnose and treat conditions that women experience. In some areas of the country, these physicians are considered specialists. However, since many women visit an obstetrician or gynecologist for routine care, some health plans consider them primary care.

Primary Caregiver = Better Managed Care

Managed care executives have pointed out that the primary care physicians control 75 to 80 percent of the dollars spent in health care. These physicians don't receive all that money themselves, but they control where it is spent.

Primary care physicians order lab tests, CT scans, MRI scans, and dozens of other tests when diagnosing illnesses. It is the primary care physician who determines whether a patient's condition requires the care of a specialist or whether a patient is sick enough to be referred to a hospital for inpatient care. The primary care physician also usually decides how long a patient should remain in the hospital.

Managed care organizations have learned that the large proportion of visits to physicians are for minor medical conditions—as much as 75 percent of all medical care is provided by primary care physicians. It is the primary care physician who is best trained for cost-effective diagnosis and treatment of these illnesses. Your primary physician can quickly determine whether your symptoms indicate a minor self-correcting problem or a condition that will need medical or surgical specialist care.

In addition to treating minor medical conditions, well-trained primary care physicians can also manage some of the more challenging medical conditions just as effectively as specialists can, yet they typically use fewer medical resources than their specialist counterparts to achieve comparable results.

Managed care plans are concerned with the health risks of overtreatment. Invasive procedures are more dangerous than non-invasive procedures. And there are risks associated with certain diagnostic tests. Health plans look to your primary care physician to assist them in selecting the most appropriate procedures and diagnostic tests that will give the most practical results while minimizing the risks associated with them.

Hospital inpatient services are even more risky, and are more costly than some of the high-tech outpatient tests. If an HMO member can be treated as an outpatient, efficiency is improved, patient satisfaction improves, and effectiveness usually remains the same. In the Rand Health Insurance Experiment, conducted by the Rand Corporation based in Santa Monica, California, researchers identified that HMO primary care physicians successfully reduced the number of members admitted to the hospital by 40 percent when compared with similar physicians practicing fee-for-service medicine. Inappropriate surgeries were also reduced. However, treatment outcomes were essentially the same.

Primary Caregiver = Medical Manager

A primary care physician is sometimes referred to as the "gatekeeper" because he or she has the power to control access to care. But the term "gatekeeper" oversimplifies what your primary care physician does. Manager over your complete health care experience, your primary care physician is your health advocate and the coordinator for all your care.

Managed care organizations need someone at the front line of care to be responsible for your welfare. These organization rely on your primary care physician's judgment to determine whether you need more specialized (and often more costly) care than he or she can provide. Figure 3-1 shows the many types of care that your primary care physician must guide you through. Without a physician acting as a clearing house for what is going on in your case, chaos would reign and your care would be haphazard at best.

The concept of a gatekeeper is not unique to our health care system. For many years primary care physicians, both HMO and non-HMO, have performed the function of controlling access to care. Physicians have the legal responsibility to

Prevention and education
  Urgent care/immediate care
    Routine ambulatory medicine/outpatient care
      Diagnosis or treatment by ancillary services
        Acute inpatient care
          Intensive care/tertiary care
            Sub-acute skilled nursing
              Home nursing
                Retirement living
                  Assisted living
                    Long term
                      Hospice

FIGURE 3-1   The continuum of care managed by the primary care physician.

control access to prescription medications. Most hospitals will not perform procedures without a physician's order.

Some physicians have performed other management functions such as coordinating care, monitoring the continuity of care, educating patients, and promoting prevention. So what is different about primary care physicians within a managed care system? First, primary care physicians now must work within an entire system of care where other caregivers have an equal stake in the outcomes. Second, managing the entire spectrum of care is not optional depending upon the personal interests of your physician. Third, your physician is probably supervised by a medical director.

Some HMO primary care physicians are free to prescribe just about anything they judge to be necessary for your care. Other primary care physicians work with more limitations placed upon them, such as a physician who is new to managed care or a physician just out of a training program. It is also true in managed care organizations that maintain tight, centralized control over utilization.

WHAT YOU SHOULD KNOW ABOUT PHYSICIAN EXTENDERS

Another difference between the past and the present in managed care is that depending upon where you live some of the primary care you receive may actually be provided by someone other than your primary care physician. That's right! Physician shortages in certain isolated areas of the country have been solved by using physician assistants and nurse practitioners who are trained to care for minor medical conditions under the supervision of a physician.

Called *physician extenders,* these licensed health care professionals may have the authority to prescribe certain medications and treatments. Trained to identify serious symptoms, they routinely review their work with a supervising primary care physician. They are educators giving you helpful self-care information to assist you in getting well at home. They can act as your advocate to the physician.

This concept is now being tested in larger multispecialty medical groups that have a high volume of HMO patients with minor ailments. In these situations physician assistants, sometimes called "PAs" and nurse practitioners, are simply the first line of diagnosis and treatment. If they find something more serious, they get your primary care physician involved immediately. They do not replace your physician for conditions needing a physician's skill and knowledge.

THE MEDICAL DIRECTOR

The health plan's medical director continually monitors the behavior of physicians under his or her supervision. This is accomplished through auditing patient charts and evaluating reports that show what types of services the physicians order for patients. Through this monitoring activity, the medical director attempts to identify which methods of treatment have proven most useful to patients as well as inappropriate medical decisions that adversely affect patients.

With statistical reports in hand, the medical director needs only a few months to develop a profile on any HMO physician. The medical director will know which physicians have an unusual pattern of inappropriate clinical decisions. This information is then used to educate physicians on how to improve their work. Physician profiling is one method health plans use to weed out physicians who either cannot or will not change their practice patterns to include more cost-effective and medically appropriate care.

Health plan medical directors guide the whole organization toward higher and higher quality of care. If a question arises regarding the most appropriate care, the medical director may get involved as an advisor. He or she may appoint one or more specialists to be consultants in your case.

Your medical director also takes a leadership position in the following activities:

- selecting new physicians and other providers
- setting company policies that affect quality of care
- designing the benefit plan
- participating on the utilization management committee

PRIMARY CARE IN RURAL AREAS

In larger cities HMOs have little difficulty in finding primary care physicians to care for HMO members; in fact, almost all primary care is provided by primary care physicians.

If you live in a rural area or a smaller town, the situation may be quite different. Here primary care is provided both by the traditional primary care physicians *and* by many specialists. This has been the case for many years because it has been difficult in these regions to recruit family physicians to move into these areas. For example, you may go to a general surgeon for primary care, or you may see a cardiologist when you have the flu. As managed care extends into smaller communities, HMOs are learning to work around this situation. They do not want to break up the physician-patient relationships.

CHAPTER 4

Medicare and Medicaid Managed Care

If I told you that this week you could get a five to ten percent discount on the food you normally purchase, I would certainly get your attention. If I told you that you could get this same discount every week on higher-quality food, you would be even more interested. While a one-time food purchase at a discount wouldn't make much of a difference to you in the long run, saving five to ten percent 52 times each year would add up to significant savings. Multiply that times ten years. Now think what could happen if all your friends could get the same discount. The savings for the whole group would be tremendous.

What does this have to do with managed care? Managed care organizations sell a lot of high-quality health care services at a discount every day. Combined, state and federal government is the largest purchaser of health care in America. Government purchases of health care account for more than 200 billion dollars annually. When government can save 10 or 20 billion dollars each year, do you think it will be interested? Absolutely! Given managed care organization's ability to deliver quality care at an affordable price it is no wonder that state and federal government health programs are interested. As taxpayers, we should be interested in this issue because it is our billions of dollars that are being spent.

There are many government-sponsored health service programs, but the two that are the most interested in managed care are Medicare (for senior citizens) and Medicaid (for the poor). If you or someone you know is a beneficiary under one of these programs you should know about your managed care options. The information in this book will help you make an informed choice.

MEDICARE MANAGED CARE

Senior citizens are the most experienced health care consumers in America. If you are a senior, you have probably been to the physician and the hospital more times than you would have preferred. Unfortunately, as we age, our body systems need more and more medical attention.

Almost three million seniors in 41 of the 50 states are members of HMOs, the majority being in Arizona, California, Florida, Illinois, Massachusetts, Minnesota, New York, Ohio, Oregon, Texas, Washington, and Wisconsin. While this is a small proportion of the total senior population over the age of 65, in the areas where HMOs for seniors are the most competitive as much as 45 percent of the seniors are members.

Under fee-for-service Medicare you probably have both Part A and Part B. Part A Medicare is hospital insurance that helps you pay for inpatient hospital care and skilled nursing facility care. Part B helps you pay for physician care and a variety of other medical services such as physical therapy, occupational therapy, speech therapy, and mental health services.

Each year under fee-for-service Medicare when you see a physician you have to pay the first $100 for services covered by Medicare. After you pay the first $100 you must pay the physician 20 percent of what Medicare approves for medical services that you receive during the rest of the year. This sounds simple enough, but add the other regulations regarding limitations on physician's charges, intermediaries, how much your doctor can charge, and the challenge of understanding all of this can be overwhelming. Enroll in a managed care plan and most, if not all, of the confusing paper work will disappear.

The federal government has established the opportunity for seniors to enroll in what it calls "coordinated care plans." This is the government's term for managed care organizations designed to care for Medicare beneficiaries.

Why Seniors Like Managed Care

Why do seniors switch to managed care? Here are some of the more popular reasons:

1. Cost. If you are a senior, you may find that switching from traditional Medicare to an HMO will save you money. In some highly competitive areas, you do not have to pay any monthly premiums. Deductibles and co-payments are very low. In most plans 100 percent of hospital care is paid for by the plan. If you are on a fixed social security income, this can make a big difference each month.
2. Fixed out-of-pocket expenses. Not only are the costs lower than with traditional Medicare program, costs for physician's visits, hospital visits, deductibles, prescriptions, and so forth are known in advance. Knowing this information can help you predict how much your health care will cost you each month.

3. The same basic coverage. All HMOs that are available to seniors must offer the same basic benefit package as you would get if you stayed with your traditional Medicare program.

4. Expanded benefits. Many managed care plans for seniors add benefits that you are unable to get through the traditional Medicare program. Depending on the health plan, these extra benefits may include hearing aids, prescription eye glasses, dental care, prescription drugs, and preventive care.

5. Simplified paperwork. By joining an HMO you greatly reduce or even eliminate the need to fill out complex forms.

6. No denial for pre-existing conditions. Except for rare situations (such as permanent kidney failure), you cannot be denied coverage because of a pre-existing condition.

7. Access to quality care. Under the Medicare program you usually can find a physician who will care for you.

8. Reduced fear of being dropped from the HMO. If you sign up with an HMO, you cannot be dropped from the plan simply because of your medical condition or the type of care that you need. This does not mean that every medical condition is paid for by the plan. In some cases, even though you may not be dropped by the plan, you may still have to pay for certain services out of your own money. Be careful, however, to read the benefit agreement. Also, be aware that if your health plan requires a monthly premium, you may be disenrolled if you fail to pay the premium.

9. Coordination of care. In most managed care programs, the care you need will be coordinated for you whether you are an inpatient or an outpatient. While you should still be involved in your care, someone from the health plan or medical group will be there to help you make the arrangements for the care you need. This can be a big help especially if you are not familiar with the different health care organizations available for your care.

10. No supplemental insurance needed. When you sign up with an HMO, you probably will not need supplemental insurance (sometimes called "Medigap" insurance) since the HMO covers almost everything. If you enroll in a Medicare HMO, you probably will be required to give up any supplemental medical insurance policy that you have. To be sure, check with your health plan representative.

11. Quality control. Managed care organizations are different from traditional health insurance companies in that they use quality control in the selection of physicians and hospitals. These organizations also use quality control principles to recommend the best diagnostic tests and treatment options available to you.

12. Freedom to change. If you do not like the managed care plan you enroll with, you have the right to go back on fee-for-service Medicare Part A and

Part B program. Or, you can change to another managed care organization that is offered in your area.

13. Right of appeal. If the managed care organization does not reimburse you for the costs of care or refuses to give you the care that you believe is medically necessary or that you are entitled to under Medicare, you have the right to appeal this decision.

14. Access to health promotion and disease prevention services. Managed care organizations have incentives to keep their members healthy and to treat illnesses quickly before the condition gets serious. By joining a managed care plan you will have access to a variety of health promotion services, such as health education programs and screening programs.

15. Fewer days in the hospital. Managed care is known for its ability to shorten the time you must spend in the hospital. To most seniors this is welcome news since they prefer to return home from the hospital as soon as possible.

Social HMOs

Among all the managed care plans for Medicare, the social HMO is one of the pilot programs that continues to show good results for the federal government. Sam Ervin, CEO of SCAN Health Plan, the nation's largest social HMO, says that

> the main difference between the typical senior plan and the social HMO is the addition of home-based and community-based long-term care services with care coordination or case management. In the social HMO we not only provide for the medical needs of the elderly, we also provide for the daily living needs of our members. Our case managers make arrangements for transportation to the beauty salon and to the grocery store if need be. If the member cannot get out of the house we make arrangements for someone to buy food and bring it to them. We will take a member to the physician's office. We make arrangements for meals to be delivered to their home. We have a friendly visitor program and a telephone contact program that gives assurance to our members that someone is watching out for them all the time whether they are well or ill.

MEDICAID MANAGED CARE

In the last decade, state Medicaid expenses have risen faster than the growth in enrollment in Medicaid fee-for-service programs. Comprising between 15 and 18 percent of most state budgets, health care services paid for by Medicaid are the fastest growing budget item in most states. And this is not because of the fact that more people are enrolled than ever before. It is because utilization of services is not under control. Some levels of care, such as the hospital emergency room, are used too frequently by many Medicaid beneficiaries. At other levels, such as primary care, physician's services are not used enough.

Currently about eight million Medicaid recipients are now members of managed care organizations in 26 states. This is expected to change dramatically during the next decade as state legislatures struggle to rein in climbing health care costs and balance state budgets. States who want to add managed care are hoping that 50 percent or more of all beneficiaries will be enrolled in one or more managed care plans. This could mean that by the year 2000 there will be as many as 20 million Medicaid beneficiaries enrolled in HMOs.

Some Medicaid managed care plans focus on specific categories of people, such as women and children. This means that you may be denied eligibility into a Medicaid HMO because of the category of aid you are in at the time you want to enroll. Check with your local state department of health or department of social services to find out if you are eligible for an HMO.

Medicaid managed care plans are adding more services at no extra charge. Medicaid HMO members can get these extras in the form of services such as transportation to the physician's office or educational programs.

Why State Governments Like Managed Care

Cost savings is one obvious reason—and in some areas of the country this alone is the significant reason—why state governments are interested in HMOs. But there is more to health care than cost. Most state legislatures are willing to privatize health care services because of the ability of private organizations to streamline administrative functions.

State laws mandate that a certain level of quality will be maintained for state-funded care. Managed care organizations offer the ability to create the desired level of quality across a wide geographic area. HMOs have the credentialling systems, authorization systems, and the emphasis on prevention that state governments like.

Perhaps the most important reason state governments like managed care is its ability to improve access to care. Patient advocacy groups have pushed for better access for years and under managed care systems this has been achieved.

Under traditional fee-for-service Medicaid arrangements you will have a difficult time finding a physician who is willing to provide your health care services. Fee-for-service payment to physicians traditionally has been low. The amount of paperwork and hassle involved in submitting claims is high. Managed care reduces these problems from the consumer's point of view. Physicians who are given a chance to share in the financial savings generated by Medicaid managed care are more willing to provide care when they get paid faster and with less hassle.

Challenges Still Exist in Medicaid

In spite of the benefits that managed care offers Medicaid programs, there are still significant challenges to overcome. For example, in some states where administrative difficulties have slowed payments to primary care physicians, some physicians simply stop accepting new Medicaid HMO members. This defeats one of the central purposes of managed care—improved access to primary care physicians.

Another challenge is the difficulty in knowing exactly who is eligible for services each month. One month you may be employed and have health insurance from your employer. The next month you may be laid off and signed up for the Medicaid HMO. Two months later you may be back at work under a new health plan.

When you enroll in managed care voluntarily, you tend to go in with your eyes open, knowing what to expect. When state Medicaid programs require you to join a prepaid health plan, you are at the mercy of individuals who enroll you and guide you through the system. And, you may feel less inclined to follow the structured relationship that the managed care organization establishes with you. The information in this book will help to guide you through the system in which you are enrolled. In addition, Figure 4-1 lists organizations to contact for more information about Medicare and Medicaid managed care.

For more information on managed care organizations in your area designed for Medicare and Medicaid populations, contact the following organizations:

For Medicare Managed Care Organizations
1. U.S. Department of Health And Human Services
   Health Care Financing Administration
   Office of Prepaid Health Care
   330 Independence Avenue, SW
   Washington, D.C. 20201
2. Social Security Administration
   1-800-638-6833
3. Your local Social Security office. Ask to speak to someone about managed care, coordinated care plans, or health maintenance organizations. Ask for a copy of the *Medicare Handbook.*
4. Your local hospital or medical society.

For Medicaid Managed Care Organizations
1. The local office of your state department of health services. Ask to speak to the office in charge of managed care.
2. The local office of your state department of social services or welfare department. Ask to speak to the office in charge of managed care.
3. Your local hospital. Ask to speak with the hospital administration or business office.

FIGURE 4-1   Where to get more information about Medicare and Medicaid managed care.

Choosing and Using an HMO

CHAPTER 5

Choosing and Enrolling in an HMO

The choice of which HMO to enroll in or even whether to enroll in one is often made for you if your employer is paying most of the bill. You will have different options depending upon your employment situation: Smaller companies may offer just one health plan. If this is your situation, your choice is whether to sign up with the health plan or not.

Larger organizations may offer more than one health plan from which to choose. If you own your own business and purchase your own health plan, you may have more than one option. Finally, if you are on Medicare or Medicaid you may have more than one alternative. Use the information in this book to make an informed decision.

So what are the things to look for when deciding which health plan to select?

A SIMPLE DECISION, A COMPLEX DECISION

No two staff model HMOs are identical and no two IPA model HMOs are the same. In any given city one HMO model may or may not outperform any of the other HMO models. Even if the premium prices of two competing plans are identical there are other more subtle differences between them.

In this chapter I outline ten decision factors that you can use to compare health plans as you make your decision. These include reputation, cost, degree of choice, benefit plan, access to care, convenience, organizational structure, utilization management, quality, and responsiveness to members. The relative importance of each factor is left for you to decide.

The information you may find for each of the ten decision factors comes from a variety of sources. Some questions are best asked of health plan representatives. Other questions should be asked of the state department of insurance, or editors of newspapers and magazines. You will want to talk with your doctor, your friends, an employer, and others. Read reports published by the health plan, by independent research groups, and the government. Or, you can talk with the local hospital administration and the medical society.

Here are the important questions to ask when evaluating the alternatives.

Reputation

1. In general, what is the reputation of the health plan in this community? If this is a new HMO, what is the overall reputation of the physicians and hospitals who have signed up with it?
2. What do health professionals say about it?
3. What do health plan members say about their own HMOs?
4. What stories have been published in local newspapers or magazines regarding the health plan?
5. What does independent research say about the reputation of HMOs in your area? In some cities, independent market research companies have studied the health plans and health care providers (physicians and hospitals). Also, in some cities independent publishing companies have created a comparison shopper's guide to HMOs.
6. What do your friends and neighbors say about it?
7. What do business leaders say about it?
8. What does the federal and state government say about it? They are careful not to recommend one HMO over others. However, they will give you more information to help you make a wise choice.
9. How long has the HMO been in business? Was it formerly known by another name and, if so, what was the reputation of the former company? Why was the name changed?
10. How many people are enrolled in the plan you are interested in?
11. Is the health plan growing? What is its growth rate?

Cost

1. How does this health plan compare on price? Monthly premiums? Annual deductible? Copayments? (See Chapter 18.)
2. What are your out-of-pocket costs for each of the plan designs offered by the HMO? If you are employed, what portion of the premium does your company pay? What portion do you pay? How does this compare with other health plans available to you?
3. What is the annual deductible for yourself? For your family? You pay the deductible only if you use covered health care services.

4. How much are the copayments that you have to pay each time you visit your physician? Hospital? Emergency room care?
5. What medical services do you anticipate using during the next twelve months?

Degree of Choice

1. When you look at the health plan provider directory, do you feel that you have sufficient freedom of choice among providers?
2. Is your current family physician listed in the health plan provider directory?
3. If your current physician is not in the provider directory, why? Is it possible for your physician to be added to the list? Does your physician want to be a provider for this health plan?
4. Is there a variety of choices for hospital care?
5. How large is the panel of specialists? Do these specialists have positive reputations in your community? How much do you know about these specialists?

Benefit Plan

1. Does the HMO offer what you need for health care coverage? Use the checklist in Figure 5-1 to assist you in evaluating the benefit plan.
2. Are any pre-existing conditions excluded from your benefits? A pre-existing condition is a medical condition that you have before enrolling in the health plan. You want the HMO to cover the health concerns you already have.
3. Are flexible benefits available? Can you customize the benefit structure in a way that will minimize your financial risk of paying more money out of your own pocket?
4. What are the limitations on benefits? For example, if you need skilled nursing facility care, is there a maximum number of days that the health plan will pay for?
5. Does the benefit agreement state under what conditions you can be disenrolled from the plan? To be disenrolled means that you no longer receive benefits because you are no longer a member of the health plan. If so, what are these conditions?
6. How does the benefit plan compare with other health plans on prescription medications? Vision care? Dental care? Long-term care?

When evaluating your HMO's benefit plan, look for the following:

1. What types of illnesses and injuries are covered?
2. What exclusions apply to certain illnesses or injuries?
3. What maximum limits apply?
4. What services are paid for?

_____ Home health care	Limitations:_____
_____ Skilled nursing	Limitations:_____
_____ Outpatient diagnostic services	Limitations:_____
_____ Surgery	Limitations:_____
_____ Prescription medications	Limitations:_____
_____ Vision care	Limitations:_____
_____ Dental care	Limitations:_____

5. What services are expressly excluded?
6. Does the health plan pay 100% of the cost of services?
7. For what services or products do you have to pay a portion of the cost out of your own pocket?

Service/Product	Amount you pay
Physician's office visits	_____
In-patient care	_____
Prescription medicines	_____
Durable medical equipment	_____
Other	_____

8. Are any pre-existing conditions excluded? Which ones?
9. Are there any permanent exclusions?
10. Is there a waiting period before coverage begins?
11. If you became seriously ill and need extended care for many months, will the health plan pay for this? For how many days or months will the health plan pay for long-term care? Does the health plan have the option of dropping you from membership if you need long-term care?
12. What procedures must be followed in a medical emergency? Where can you go for care? Who must be called for authorization? What is the telephone number?

FIGURE 5-1   Benefit checklist.

Access to Care

1. How accessible is your primary care physician when you need an appointment, or another primary care physician if your physician is not available? How accessible are the specialists?
2. What is the average length of time patients wait in the reception room? On the average, how long does the physician spend with each patient?

3. Are extended hours available for physician visits? If so, what are they?
4. Are you able to see the same primary care physician each time you schedule a routine appointment?
5. Are second opinions available? Under what conditions?
6. What is the HMO's policy regarding out-of-town care?
7. For what specific kinds of procedures is authorization required? How long does the authorization process take for special procedures?
8. If you are admitted to the hospital, which physician will admit you and follow your care? Is it your primary care physician or a different physician who does mainly the hospital work?

Convenience

1. Is one-stop shopping available for all or most services? Is the clinic location near where you work or live?
2. What is the location for primary care? Urgent care? Specialty care? Ancillary services (X ray, laboratory, diagnostic testing, physical therapy, etc.)? Hospital care?
3. If you had to drive from one location to another on the same day, how convenient would it be for you? From home? From work?
4. If you must go to more than one facility for health care, do the people working in the system assist you in knowing what to do next, where to go, and how to interact with health care workers in other parts of the system?
5. How complex is the process to secure authorization or certification for special procedures? If there is a dispute, who has the last word on authorization requests? Will you be informed regarding the authorization on the same day that the physician is informed?
6. How much paperwork is involved for you?
7. How often will you receive formal reports (for example, written copies of laboratory reports or reports from other diagnostic tests) of your progress? How quickly will you receive results from diagnostic tests? Can you expect to receive verbal reports (telephone contact) from your physician to let you know how your treatment is progressing?
8. How convenient is the service compared to the same service offered by other health plans?

Organizational Structure

1. What type of model does the health plan use in its relationship with physicians: the staff model, group model, network model, IPA model, direct contracting model, or some other structure?

2. Does the company that owns the health plan also own the hospitals? The physician groups? The skilled nursing facilities?
3. Does the health plan or the delivery network have a computer communication system that allows someone in one part of the health plan to communicate easily with someone in another part of the plan? For example, if you go to the medical group, can someone there send information via computer to the hospital about services that you need? Can someone in the medical group make an appointment for you at the hospital?
4. How is the health plan structured internally by department? Who is in charge of claims processing? Authorization and certification? Member relations? Refer to Figure 5-2 for a list of the typical departments within a managed care organization.
5. To what degree do consumers influence the health plan's governance? Do consumers sit on the Board of Directors? If so, how many?

Administration oversees all health plan operations including the following departments.

Claims processing receives claims and pays providers or reimburses members.

Finance conducts the financial planning and reporting of all health plan activities.

Marketing and enrollment communicates with potential subscribers and facilitates the enrollment process.

Medical services oversees the clinical services such as those offered at health plan clinics and facilities.

Member services provides problem-solving assistance and guidance on how to use the health plan.

Provider relations and contracting develops and maintains productive relationships with all outside contracted physicians, hospitals, and other organizations that provide care.

Quality improvement conducts an ongoing formal review of how to improve the quality of care and of administrative services.

Regulatory compliance and government relations makes sure that the health plan maintains its licensure, certification, and accreditation.

Utilization management monitors and reports on all aspects of health care service use across all provider groups.

FIGURE 5-2 The departments within a typical managed care plan.

Utilization Management

1. How well does the health plan manage the use of health care services actually delivered to you? (See Chapter 10.)
2. Who is responsible for authorization and certification? Are the authorization requests reviewed by someone with relevant training and experience? What level of training and licensure do these individuals have? Are the authorization clerks registered nurses and licensed physicians? If you have a specialized medical need, does a qualified medical or surgical specialist get involved in the authorization process?
3. Who follows your situation to help you get the services you need in a timely basis?
4. Are health plan members encouraged to be involved in medical decisions? How?
5. Do the hospital nurses and physicians work together in following standardized procedures for care during inpatient care? Are medical practice guidelines used?
6. How do the health plan's utilization statistics on quality and responsiveness compare with national averages? With regional averages? See Table 5-1 for an example of utilization statistics.

Quality

1. Is the health plan accredited by a nationally recognized accrediting body? If so, which one?

TABLE 5-1

HMO Utilization Statistics—Average Hospital Inpatient Days per 1,000 HMO Members Compared with the Nation as a Whole, 1993

Non-Medicare Members	
U.S. national average	400/1,000 population
HMO average	296/1,000 HMO members
Some HMOs*	150/1,000 HMO members
Medicare Members	
U.S. national average	2,500/1,000 population
HMO average	1,697/1,000 HMO members
Some HMOs	1,100/1,000 HMO members

*This is an example of the levels of utilization that some health plans have achieved. Every health plan is a little different and achieves different results.

2. How often are physician credentials evaluated? Do health plan physicians submit to a thorough review of continuing training and clinical skill?
3. Does the health plan and medical group use a paperless, computerized medical record and claims system? If not, do they have plans to install such a system?
4. What is the average amount of time that health plan physicians have remained with the plan?
5. Does the health plan use formal admission criteria in deciding whether a member needs to be admitted to the hospital?
6. Does the health plan conduct an audit of a physician's ability to keep an accurate and complete medical record? If so, how often is such an audit completed?
7. What is the readmission rate within thirty days of discharge? In other words, what percent of the patients who are discharged from the hospital are readmitted within thirty days after discharge?
8. Does the health plan routinely investigate unusual events? These would include such things as death during or after surgery, return to the intensive care unit within 24 hours of being transferred out, abnormal results of diagnostic tests that are not explained in the medical record, and medical instability of a patient at the time of discharge from the hospital.
9. What are the patient satisfaction rating scores generated from surveys? What is the disenrollment rate?

Responsiveness to Members

1. How responsive is the HMO or medical group to members' concerns?
2. Does a formal member relations department exist? This is sometimes called customer service, patient relations, or member services.
3. Are customer service representatives available 24 hours a day?
4. What is the grievance procedure like? Ask to see a copy in writing before you sign up.
5. How many grievances have been filed the last 12 months? Of those files, how many have been successfully resolved?

THE ENROLLMENT PROCESS

Enrolling through Your Employer

Enrolling in the HMO of your choice is relatively easy compared with the process of evaluating the health plan. Figure 5-3 summarizes the usual steps to follow. In

1. Ask to read the promotional materials published by the health plan.
2. Ask to read the benefit agreement.
3. Ask the questions that meet your needs.
4. Talk with an enrollment representative. Verify his or her credentials.
5. When you have made your decision, complete the enrollment form with the help of the health plan enrollment representative.
6. When the health plan sends you printed information in the mail, read everything carefully. Make sure that you understand what to do in case of an emergency. Make sure that you understand the grievance process.
7. Read the benefit agreement or plan summary again. If you are still confused about anything, call the health plan for clarification.
8. Read your identification card and call your health plan to make any corrections.
9. Call the member services department of the health plan if you have any questions.
10. If you did not select a primary care physician as part of your enrollment, do so immediately.
11. Call or meet someone from the primary care physician's office.
12. If problems come up or confusion occurs, call the member services department immediately. Do not wait for problems to take care of themselves. People are busy, and you have the right to start managing your care right after you enroll.

FIGURE 5-3   The enrollment process.

addition, here are three important tips to know so that the process will go more smoothly:

1. If you are signing up through your employer, someone from your health benefits department or human resources department will give you information about the health plan and how to sign up. *Be sure to read the benefit agreement.* Ask questions about anything you may not understand. If you are asked to enroll in the plan before you have read the benefit agreement, refuse to enroll until you have actually read it.
2. Open enrollment is usually a thirty-day period when employees may elect to sign up with the health plan. Open enrollment can follow the start of employment, come at the end of the year, or take place whenever the company changes health plans. Most companies will not let you switch health plans in mid year unless you terminate your employment. So, after you sign up, you generally have one year before you are allowed to make any changes in your health plan, such as adding a new family member, changing to a point-of-service option, and so forth. If you are able to sign up a family member after the close of the open enrollment period, this family member may have to wait a few months before benefits apply to them.

3. You will receive an enrollment form that asks for basic information. All the information you provide on the enrollment form is eventually entered into the health plan's computer database. Be sure to fill in the form completely the first time. Missing information on your record may mean extra time and confusion later when you need to access it.

Enrolling in a Medicare HMO

If you are on Medicare and decide to join an HMO, your enrollment process will be a little different than it is for someone signing up at work. Medicare-approved HMOs sign up new members one at a time, not in groups. When you are ready to sign up with the health plan, a certified enrollment representative will visit you personally to help you complete the paperwork. Be sure to read the application materials carefully. *Take your time.* No one should rush you into signing up.

Before you sign up with the health plan, contact the plan and verify that the enrollment representative is a legitimate, qualified employee of the health plan.

After you sign up, it takes approximately 45 days for the health plan to submit your application to Medicare before you receive approval for your membership in the health plan. When Medicare approves your application, your name will be marked in the government's computer system and an official notification will be transmitted to your new health plan. When you are officially a member, you should receive formal notification in the form of a letter and a membership card.

Enrolling in a Medicaid HMO

If you are on Medicaid or welfare, you may have the option of signing up with an HMO. More and more states are offering this option. How you enroll, though, varies from state to state. When you want to enroll in a Medicaid-approved HMO, contact the local office of your state department of social services or your state department of health services. In some states you will be contacted by the state. You may be asked to personally visit one of these local offices to enroll in an HMO. Or, you may be asked to enroll through the mail. In other cases, you may be given the names and telephone numbers of the Medicaid-approved HMOs in your area and you are then responsible for contacting the HMO and telling them that you want to enroll.

If you choose a medical group, you still need to select a primary care physician. Do this as early as possible to prevent confusion later when you may have an urgent need to see a physician.

Some states allow a few days' grace period after signing up that allows new Medicaid HMO members to change their minds without disrupting their care. Find out how many days this period is for your area.

At the time you sign up, make sure to get the name and telephone number of the health plan representative who processed your enrollment. You may need to contact this person again later if your physician is unable to verify that you are an HMO member.

Federal Employees Health Benefit Program

The Federal Employees Health Benefits Program (FEHBP) is required to offer the ten million federal employees a choice of health plans. An increasingly popular choice is a managed care plan. If you enroll in such a plan the information in this book will be helpful to you. However, there may be differences in how your plan is administered.

Managed care organizations that serve federal employees may have to adjust their benefit plans and operations slightly compared with what is offered other groups. For example, if you are a member of the FEHBP and an HMO member, you may be able to follow a more open authorization process.

HOW TO MAKE YOUR FIRST VISITS GO SMOOTHLY

Review the Benefit Agreement

One of the most frustrating things for health plan physicians and administrators is that members do not read their benefit agreements at the time they enroll. The information contained in the benefit agreement and related materials can reduce or even eliminate the frustration that the health plan member experiences the first few times he or she uses the system. So take a few minutes to read the benefit agreement. Some of the information will be interesting and some of it will be boring, but the more familiar you are with it, the better the health plan will work for you.

In addition, W. C. Williams III, M.D., president of the National Association of Managed Care Physicians based in Virginia, believes that employers—the major purchasers of health plan services—should do more to inform employees regarding the benefit agreement. For example, employers should conduct orientation sessions for employees.

After reading your benefit information you should know where to call for assistance, where the pharmacy is located, when the clinics are open during the day, and generally how to get the most out of your health plan. Keep the information near your telephone.

Check and Use Your Membership Card

A few days after you enroll you will probably receive a membership card. In some plans, temporary paper cards are issued for your use until your permanent plastic card arrives. This card is vital to your success as a plan member. When you receive the card:

1. Confirm that the information on the card is correct. If, for example, the wrong physician's name is entered on the card, or if your name is spelled incorrectly, inform the health plan immediately to prevent confusion in the future.
2. Read the entire card on both sides. You will be surprised how much information is located there.
3. Carry your card with you at all times. Remember, you may not have had to use a health plan card like this before. Your card is one of the most important pieces of information your physician will need.
4. When you enroll in an HMO your Medicaid or Medicare card may no longer be valid. Even if you have an old card, be sure to use the health plan card when you visit your physician. This will prevent confusion and aggravation later.

Introduce Yourself to Member Services

It pays to get to know the people who will help you when you do get sick. Before you visit your primary care physician for the first time as a plan member, call the member services department and ask them a few questions to confirm what you should do under certain circumstances:

1. Introduce yourself and explain that you are calling for clarification on a number of points. These could include questions such as: What do I do in case of an emergency? What if I am out of town when I get sick? If I need medication in the middle of the night, what should I do? What do I do on weekends and in the middle of the night? How can I get advice on whether I should go to the emergency room or not?
2. Ask for additional information on health promotion classes offered in your area during the next month. Then register and attend one of the classes to get better acquainted with the health plan.

Be Prepared for Your First Physician Visit

If you visit your physician's office soon after enrolling, your physician may not have received a printed list from the health plan that contains your name. If you arrive at the physician's office and no one seems to know you, ask them to call the health plan office to verify eligibility. Your membership card is not proof of eligibility. It is simply an identification card.

In the event that your physician is unable to verify that you are eligible, immediately contact the health plan representative who enrolled you. If he or she is unavailable to help you in this situation, ask to speak with the enrollment supervisor. In this kind of situation time is usually of the essence.

If you were under the care of a specialist before changing health plans, you still need to meet the primary care physician to which you are assigned. Do not automatically go back to the specialist unless your new primary care physician authorizes you to do so.

Some health plans prefer that you visit the health plan physician for a checkup soon after you enroll.

SPECIALIZED SERVICES WITHIN MANAGED CARE

Understanding how specialized managed care programs work will help you get the most out of your relationship with your health plan. Pharmacy coverage, mental health and substance abuse care, and vision and dental treatment are managed differently from traditional health care, and services vary from HMO to HMO.

Managed Pharmacy Care

Medications are a vital part of the health care plan that your physician prescribes. As costs for medicines continue to rise, many managed care organizations are developing special programs to manage quality and costs. Here are some things to be aware of regarding how pharmacy products and services work under managed care:

- Your health plan may have developed a list of medicines, called the *formulary,* from which physicians may choose when prescribing medications.
- If a formulary is used, any request for a medicine that is not on the list may need to be authorized like any other special procedure.
- You may have to go to a designated pharmacy to have your prescriptions filled.
- If your physician writes a prescription for an over-the-counter medication, you normally must pay for that out of your own pocket.
- Only a prescription written by a health plan physician may be paid for.

- You may be required to pay a portion of the medication's cost out of your own pocket.
- Sometimes brand name medications are not listed in the formulary when their generic brand equivalents are listed. If you prefer brand name medications when generic brands are available, you may be required to pay the difference in cost between the generic brand and the name brand.
- When you go to a designated pharmacy, your membership eligibility may be checked just as it will be if you go to a hospital for care.
- Your health plan may offer you a mail order pharmacy service if you must continue taking medicine over a long period of time.
- Medicines that your health plan considers experimental or unproven may not be approved under your benefit agreement.
- There may be other limitations on the use of pharmacy products. Be sure to ask your health plan representative for information regarding what is covered in your pharmacy benefits.

Mental Health and Substance Abuse Care

Care for mental health and substance abuse is an area of great interest in managed care organizations. Organizations which must comply with government regulations on the minimum benefits that must be offered are trying to find creative ways to manage this type of care.

Some managed care organizations delegate a portion of your care to a group that specializes in mental health and substance abuse. In this case you would deal with your health plan for medical problems and with another organizations for mental health issues.

Managed Vision Care and Dental Care

Benefits for vision care and dental care are not automatically part of your benefit agreement unless your employer chooses to add them to the managed care plan that is purchased. Be aware that there may be benefit limitations to these care options just as there are with the rest of your health coverage. There is also a list of preferred providers who are under contract with the health plan that you must use. The process of getting authorization for these services varies from health plan to health plan. Check with your health plan for how these issues are covered.

Following these suggestions and having this information will make it easier for you to have a positive experience with your managed care plan. After you have asked your questions, use Figure 5-4, the sample summary decision sheet, to compare your evaluation of the various alternatives.

After you gather information about an HMO, complete the chart below. For each *factor*, assign a percent *weight* based on how important each item is to your final decision. For example, if you think that cost is slightly more important than access, give cost a higher percent weight. The total percent weight should be 100%. If you want to leave out one or more factors, just assign a zero to the weight of the one(s) you want to leave out. To be fair in your comparison of alternate health plans, use the same weight percentages for each health plan.

Then give a *rating* to each factor of the alternative HMOs and health plans from which you are choosing. The rating of each factor is your estimate of how attractive the health plan is on the factor.

Use the following rating scale:

1 = Poor rating
2 = Mediocre rating
3 = Average rating
4 = Above average rating
5 = Superior rating

To get the *score* for each factor, multiply the weight of each item by the rating you assigned it. Add up the scores for the factors to produce a *total score*. Compare the total score of one health plan with the total score of another health plan.

Factor	Weight		Rating		Score
Reputation	15%	x	4	=	0.60
Cost	20%	x	3	=	0.60
Degree of choice	15%	x	5	=	0.75
Benefit plan	10%	x	3	=	0.30
Access	5%	x	4	=	0.20
Convenience	5%	x	4	=	0.20
Organizational structure	2%	x	3	=	0.06
Utilization management	5%	x	3	=	0.15
Quality	15%	x	3	=	0.45
Responsiveness	8%	x	4	=	0.32
Total score	100%				3.78

Based on personal judgment, this HMO receives a score of 3.78 (almost a 4 on the scale of 1 to 5), or just above average. A perfect score would be 5.0. Compare this score with the score you would get from evaluating another HMO, and remember that these numbers are merely examples.

FIGURE 5-4 Sample summary decision sheet.

C H A P T E R 6

Choosing a Good Physician and Hospital

When you enroll in a managed care organization, it would be best if you could keep the physician you are already using. Unfortunately, you may find that when you receive the list of providers during the enrollment process, your favorite physician is not on the list. You may find that your physician, for one reason or another, is resisting the invitations of your health plan to join. Or maybe you have been going to a specialist for primary care and this specialist is not eligible to be a primary care physician.

YOU DO HAVE A CHOICE

Whether you receive care in the setting of an HMO or through private health insurance, you choose your physician. You decide whether to discharge your physician and select another *at will.*

As you get older or as you experience more health problems, your choice of physicians becomes more important. Younger, healthier HMO members may have an easier time choosing a new physician since they need one less frequently. If you are an older HMO member, your choice of physician and hospital can be the determining factor in whether you sign up with the HMO in the first place. One thing will probably never change when it comes to choosing the right health plan: when you have a good family physician, it doesn't really matter which health plan you belong to.

SELECTING YOUR PRIMARY CARE PHYSICIAN

Selecting an HMO physician is sometimes done in the privacy of your own home. You have a printed list of physicians on the table. How do you decide which physician is best for you? Some people prefer to simply pick a name from the printed list. Some will ask a friend or relative for a recommendation. If you are the type of person who needs more information before selecting a physician, here are some suggestions:

1. Make a game plan to guide you in your selection. Start by making a list of questions you want to ask directly of the physician.
2. Telephone the physician's office. By calling on the telephone you can judge how interested the HMO employees are in welcoming new members. Does their tone of voice tell you that they are eager to talk with you? Are they courteous to you? Do they have specific information on how well the physician keeps his or her appointments? Is the physician available to talk to you on the telephone if you have questions between visits? Are they interested in answering your questions as you try to decide which physician is best for you?
3. Talk with other people who are members of the same health plan. Ask them to describe their primary care physician. Many of these people have had personal experience with the physicians on your list. They don't have any axe to grind on the physician's behalf; they can tell you how it really is.
4. Talk with medical or nursing professionals. They see the HMO physicians on a daily basis. They know which physicians are the most personable and popular. They watch the physician while he or she is at the hospital bed side. They know which physicians wait until late at night to make hospital rounds and which physicians visit their hospital patients earlier in the day.
5. Narrow your selection down to two or three names and then ask to meet these physicians in person. Physicians are busy people, but so are you. Why not minimize the risk of having to change physicians at a later date by meeting the physicians for a few minutes before you make your final selection? If you hired a building contractor to install a new kitchen or bathroom, wouldn't you expect to meet the person in charge of the project before you engaged them in professional services? If you needed a lawyer, wouldn't you interview the person before retaining him or her? By meeting with a physician personally you are selecting an individual who carries the professional responsibility of assisting you in a vital concern—managing your health.
6. If you already have a primary care physician but need specialist care, the primary care physician has a lot of influence in selecting the physician he or she believes is best for you. This does not mean that you have no choice in the matter. Ask to talk with the recommended specialist either on the telephone or in person. If you are having elective surgery, you should take the time to speak with the surgeon. If time is of the essence, as in a medical emergency, this may not be an option.

7. Where is the physician located? Is this convenient for you or those who transport you if you travel from home? From work? What are the office hours during the week? On the weekends?

8. When interviewing potential new physicians, here are some questions to ask:

    a. Does the primary care physician have a specialty? If so, what is it? Don't assume that a physician listed as a primary care physician doesn't have a specialty. When signing up with a health plan some physicians who have training in a specialty, such as cardiology, simply put "internal medicine" when asked what specialty they have. Of course, this is correct.

      Also ask if the physician is board certified in a primary care specialty. Don't hesitate to get specific information about the physician. If you are not sure whether the physician's training is in primary care, ask for clarification but do not assume that the enrollment representative knows the subtle differences among physicians. Call the health plan credentials department or provider relations department to get the information you need.

    b. Who covers for the physician when he or she is sick or on vacation? Do not accept a general answer such as "your physician will find a good physician to fill in when he is gone on vacation."

    c. If your first language is something other than English, does the physician speak the language? If English is the physician's second language, can you understand the physician when he or she speaks?

    d. Where did the physician go to medical school? What hospital did the physician train at during a residency program? If you are concerned about choosing a physician who was trained in another country, you should know the background of your physician before you sign up.

    e. If you have a chronic medical condition or a family history of certain illnesses, ask whether the physician you are interested in has specific experience treating these conditions.

    f. If the physician, the office staff, or the HMO enrollment staff seem irritated at your inquiries, tell them that selecting a physician is more important than almost all other choices that you will make in the health plan. Then ask to speak to the director of member services to air your concerns.

    g. With which hospitals is the physician affiliated?

    h. How do you get in touch with your physician in an emergency?

    i. How much experience has the physician had with the HMO? If it is less than $1\frac{1}{2}$ years, the physician is still learning and adjusting to the HMO. If the physician is new to this HMO, ask whether he or she has experience working with other managed care organizations and if so, which

1. Establish a game plan before you choose your captain.
2. Review the provider list supplied by your health plan.
3. Talk with informed people before making your final selections.
4. Narrow your selections down to two or three names.
5. Find out the location and office hours of each physician.
6. Conduct your own investigation of each physician on your list.
7. Have a short face-to-face interview with the physicians.
8. Determine the personal qualities that are important to you such as compassion, interest, warmth, thoroughness, ability to communicate, and so forth.
9. Make your selection.
10. Make an initial visit to the physician you have chosen.
11. Give the relationship a fair chance to succeed. Become an active participant in the physician-patient relationship.
12. Be willing to make a change if necessary, but avoid changing physicians too often. This disrupts the continuity of care.

FIGURE 6-1   Checklist for selecting a physician.

ones and for how long? Also, if the physician speaks derogatorily about the HMO this could signal a lack of interest in participating in managed care.

  j. How many different HMOs does the physician belong to? If you or your employer decides at a later date to change health plans, you may have to change physicians.

9. Ask to see the patient satisfaction survey results naming specific physicians. Compare what you find on the survey results with what others say about the physician.

Use the checklist in Figure 6-1 when selecting a managed care physician.

Your First Visit to Your Physician

Whether you are are ill or not, you should visit your primary care physician soon after enrolling. Getting a complete medical history will help your physician begin managing your care right from the start. If you have a chronic condition or use any type of durable medical equipment, the health plan and the medical group will want to know about this. If your health plan does not encourage you to visit your new physician soon after signing up, make the appointment without their suggestion. As you prepare for this first visit, keep the following suggestions in mind:

1. If you changed physicians when joining the health plan, ask your previous physician to send a copy of your medical records to the new health plan

physician. (Figure 6-2 shows a sample letter of request.) You should not have to apologize for or defend your reason for making such a simple request. Be prepared to make the request in writing since your previous physician will need legal record of your request. The following are among the reasons you can give your previous physician:

a. You want to enhance continuity of care.
b. You need to reduce the amount of time you have to spend undergoing diagnostic tests and physical examinations that have already been performed at your previous physician's request.
c. You want to prevent an inconvenience to the physician in case there is a medical emergency.

Dear Dr. Jones,

I want to thank you for providing excellent care to me and my family during the past few years/months. We appreciate your personal attention when we have needed it.

As you know, I have signed up with the (insert name) managed care plan through (insert employer, Medicare HMO, or Medicaid HMO name). I was disappointed to learn that you are not a provider for this health plan. During the enrollment process I was asked to select a new primary care physician who is a designated provider. I have selected

Dr. John Doe
1234 Main Street #123
Anytown, ST 12345

As part of the process of starting my care with the new health plan, I request that you send a copy of my medical record or a summary of my current health status to Dr. Doe as soon as possible. I am scheduled to visit Dr. Doe on (insert date). My records will encourage continuity of care and give the physician helpful information in case there is a medical emergency. Sending the records now will prevent an inconvenience later in case medical tests are required. Therefore, I am giving my permission for you to release my medical record to Dr. Doe. I will gladly reimburse you for the cost of copying and mailing the report to Dr. Doe.

If you have any questions, please do not hesitate to call me any time. Thank you for your help with this.

Sincerely,

(Your name)

FIGURE 6-2 Sample letter of request for medical records to be sent to your new physician.

d. If you have a chronic condition, this is all the more reason why your new physician needs to have your current medical records as soon as possible.

e. You may need to participate in a special case management program right from the start and the new physician needs the information.

Keep in mind that the medical records your physician keeps are records about you. You have legal right to have a copy of the information contained in the records and to give it to whomever you wish.

2. When making your first appointment, explain clearly what you want. If you are simply introducing yourself to the physician, tell this to the clerk. Explain that you want to get acquainted with the physician and to complete the medical history form. The scheduling clerk may ask about symptoms or complaints. This is a routine question that helps the office determine how quickly they should work you into their schedule. Do not expect to spend a long time with the physician on this introductory visit; he or she will have a full schedule treating sick patients. But do not apologize for making this visit. Even though you feel well now, there is nothing wrong with getting acquainted with the physician before you need medical services.

3. If you make your first appointment because of an illness, explain your symptoms to the nurse or scheduling clerk. Make a list of the symptoms you experience. Note where your pain is located, on what occasions or how often you feel the pain, and how severe the pain is. See Figure 6-3 and 6-4 for more ideas on how to prepare for the visit.

4. The medical history and physical examination are two of the most vital procedures that your primary care physician performs before he or she can provide care. Insiders call this history and physical the "H & P." The medical history is both a written form you will be asked to complete as well as an interview by the physician. The physical exam is an evaluation of your overall state of health. It may be a simple exam or a comprehensive exam.

5. Tell your physician about all medications you take, including over-the-counter medications you buy without a prescription. Glenn Spielman, director of Member Services for the Geisinger Health Plan in Danville, Pennsylvania, suggests that on your first visit to your HMO physician, bring in a brown bag of all the medications that you take. Let your physician discuss each medication with you. If you have concerns about side effects of these medications, ask for an explanation. If you are concerned that you are taking too many medications, ask your physician how you can reduce the number.

6. If you have been seeing a specialist on a regular basis (every month or every few weeks), mention this to your HMO primary care physician. Then discuss the situation with your physician. As a new member, you must discuss the situation with your primary care physician before you continue

If you are ill, take a few minutes to complete this form. Thinking about these questions before the physician sees you will help you give more complete information.

1. What are your symptoms? Be prepared to give specific information.
2. Describe your pain. Where is the pain located? How often do you feel the pain? What type of pain is it?
3. What current medications has a physician prescribed for you? Include all over-the-counter medications that you buy without a prescription.

Drug name	How many times a day?	How long have you been taking it?	For what illness?
_____	_____	_____	_____
_____	_____	_____	_____

4. What have you done to care for yourself since you first noticed the symptoms? With what results? Be specific.
5. Have you seen a physician for this condition before? If so, when? What was done for you? What results were achieved?
6. What is your family history of similar conditions?
7. What exposures to harmful substances have you had? Where do you work? What kinds of occupational hazards do you know exist for your work? Do you smoke? Do you drink? Do you use harmful drugs?
8. Have you noticed any changes in your physical activity? Elimination? Breathing patterns? Heart rate? Emotional state? Diet or appetite? Sleep pattern? Overall energy level?
9. Are you organized in monitoring your symptoms? Do you have the required equipment and notebook available? Do you have a log book? Do you have a place for the physician to write down his or her instructions?
10. To what degree are you willing or able to participate in the decision making regarding the best course of treatment? If you are unable, will someone assist you in medical decision making?
11. What special events or travel plans do you have that may affect your care or the results of your care? Tell your physician about these plans before the event.

FIGURE 6-3 Preparing to see the physician when you are ill.

seeing the specialist. Say something like, "I've been going to a cardiologist for several months and need to know whether I will be able to continue. My next scheduled appointment is in three weeks. What can we work out for this?"

CHARACTERISTICS OF GOOD HOSPITALS

Hospitals with the best name recognition are often the hospitals that HMOs turn to first when selling their health plans to a community. But name recognition is only one indicator of quality. Here are a few other indicators to watch for:

When you are ill, there are many questions you should ask your physician.

Top-Priority Questions:
1. What is causing my symptoms?
2. What will be done and why?
3. When will it be done?
4. What are the risks and benefits?
5. What alternatives exist?
6. What will it cost me in terms of time, discomfort, and money?

Additional Questions:
1. Will I get better without medical or surgical treatment?
2. Do I have a condition with hidden symptoms?
3. What will this procedure involve?
4. If the procedure is an invasive procedure, what will the recovery phase be like?
5. How often is this procedure performed?
6. What are the failure rates?
7. Who will actually perform the procedure?
8. Will a house staff physician or a physician-in-training be involved in the procedure?
9. Can I refuse to have the house staff physician involved?
10. Will blood be drawn? If so, what tests will be performed on it?
11. What other tests do I need and how accurate is the information that you get from them?
12. What medication will I need to take and what are the side effects?
13. What else do I need to know about diet, exercise, and so forth?
14. What will happen if I refuse to have this treatment?

FIGURE 6-4   Questions to ask your physician about your treatment plan.

1. A hospital that is involved with the community cannot afford to encourage poor quality. Community involvement can take many forms. Here are a few examples:
   a. Does the hospital provide free or low-cost public education programs on a variety of health topics on a regular basis?
   b. Do the hospital managers and leading physicians in the medical staff organization participate as active members in community service organizations?
   c. Does the hospital offer free or low-cost health services such as prostate screening, blood pressure screening, glaucoma screening, flu immunizations, and so forth?
   d. If you call the hospital with a health question, can you easily find someone with whom you can talk confidentially, for example, the pharmacist, the dietitian, or the physical therapist?

2. Does the hospital use up-to-date quality improvement techniques? What continuous quality improvement programs does the hospital maintain? With what results?
3. How active is the medical staff organization? Do the physicians participate in decision making? Do physicians take an active role in continuous quality improvement efforts? If so, in what ways?
4. What *quality indicators* does the hospital report to the public? A quality indicator is a measurement of how well the hospital compares to a standard or to other hospitals. Quality indicators for hospitals are similar to those produced by health plans. (See Chapter 19.) Here are just a few examples:
    a. The number of readmissions to the hospital within 24 hours of discharge from the hospital emergency room. This is an indicator of the ability of the emergency room treatment team to correctly diagnose and treat your illness.
    b. The number of emergency room patients who leave before being treated. Patients who leave before being treated generally feel that they have to wait too long.
    c. The percent of patients who need to be transferred back to the intensive care unit (ICU). If a patient is transferred out of ICU too quickly, it generally means that quality of care has suffered.
5. Do the employees of the hospital treat you with respect?
6. Does the hospital billing office prepare correct bills? Does the billing office work well with your health plan?

You can evaluate other providers of care in the same way you do physicians and hospitals. Skilled nursing facilities, surgery centers, and home nursing care are three other types of organizations that you are likely to encounter as a member of a managed care organization.

Most managed care organizations encourage members to ask questions. So even if you ask just a few questions about quality of care, in the process you will become a better informed co-captain of your managed care team.

CHAPTER 7

Promoting Health and Preventing Disease

For decades Americans have gradually increased their expectations of what medicine can do. We like to consult with our physician more frequently and regarding a wider variety of health concerns than did our grandparents. Medical miracles have convinced us that no matter what ails us, we can get relief from our physician.

During the last 20 years personal health has taken on an increased importance in our American lifestyle. People jog, walk, and cycle to stay fit. We are obsessed with losing weight and managing our stress. We watch the fat content of our diets. Millions of Americans have stopped smoking.

Independent of our physicians' medical advice, Americans are actively exploring the potential benefits of alternative therapies such as chiropractic, megavitamin therapy, homeopathy, acupuncture, biofeedback, macrobiotics, massage, spiritual healing, and self-help groups. In an attempt to deal with common health concerns such as headaches, backaches, depression, anxiety, insomnia, digestive problems and many other ailments, we are willing to spend our time and money to get relief. We still depend upon our primary care physician to diagnose, treat, and explain our maladies, but spending money on alternative therapy is often less expensive than seeing the physician. Collectively we spend over $10 billion each year on alternative therapy. This type of therapy offers a low-risk supplement to help us on our way to wellness.

PROMOTING GOOD HEALTH MUST BECOME ROUTINE

In his foreword to the U.S. government publication *Healthy People 2000* (U.S. Department of Health and Human Services, Public Health Service, 1990), Secretary Louis W. Sullivan, M.D., remarks that the American public has become "increasingly health conscious, increasingly appreciative of the extent to which our physical and emotional well-being is dependent upon measures that only we, ourselves can affect."

While to a large extent we have eradicated the crippling communicable diseases of the first half of this century, we now contend with chronic diseases, negative health consequences of social ills, and new communicable diseases for which there are no cures at present. Secretary Sullivan and the thousands of health experts who contributed to *Healthy People 2000* make the assertion that for all Americans health promotion and disease prevention are our best opportunities "to reduce the ever-increasing portion of our resources that we spend to treat preventable illness and functional impairment."

Here is some of what the health experts demonstrate in the secretary's report:

1. Preventable cancers and heart disease still rank at the top of the list of diseases from which Americans die the most often.

2. Spending just 30 minutes a day walking will improve muscle tone and preserve organ reserves for a longer, more active life. Regular exercise by older Americans is associated with stronger bones, less coronary artery disease, less hypertension, less depression and anxiety, less diabetes, and less colon cancer.

3. About 300,000 fewer people would die prematurely if no one smoked cigarettes. Cigarette smoking is still the single most important preventable cause of premature death in America.

4. If we stopped drinking alcohol excessively or entirely, 100,000 fewer people would die from auto accident injuries and homicides and from unnecessary illnesses, such as cirrhosis of the liver. Alcohol is the leading preventable cause of birth defects.

5. Limiting total dietary fat to less than 30 percent of calories will contribute to lower rates of coronary artery disease, gall bladder disease, and colon cancer.

6. The leading cause of death for children ages 1 through 14 is still injuries from automobile accidents, drownings, and fire. Violence toward children is the fastest-growing cause of injury for this age group.

7. Low birth weight is the greatest single risk factor for infant mortality in America. Yet this condition is associated with conditions that are preventable, such as cigarette smoking, lack of good prenatal medical care, alcohol and drugs, and pregnancy when the mother is younger than 18 years of age.

8. Early detection can greatly lower the risks of premature death from specific diseases such as cervical cancer, colon cancer, prostate cancer, and breast cancer.

9. Add up the costs and experts estimate that over $300 billion dollars are spent annually for diseases that are almost entirely preventable.

THE THREE ROADS TO PREVENTION

Until recently insurance companies saw their role as avoiding risk rather than managing risk. They did not pay physicians to provide health promotion or disease prevention services. Managed care organizations have gradually improved upon this. However, during the first decades of managed care prevention did not receive as much attention as it should have. Now prevention is one of the strongest areas of emphasis.

Ideally, if you change your personal behaviors you will lower your risk of the preventable, high-cost diseases—this is the first road to prevention. Through primary prevention, you increase the information you have about health and disease, make lifestyle changes that minimize the risk of getting diseases, make efforts to detect diseases early, and increase appropriate self care. Figure 7-1 depicts the three roads to prevention.

Once you are diagnosed as having a disease, it is too late for primary preven-

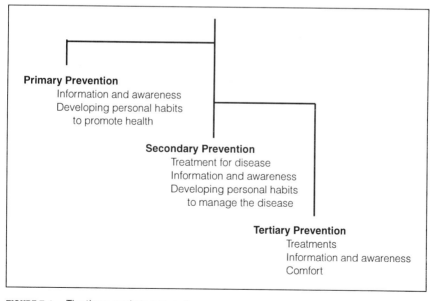

FIGURE 7-1   The three roads to prevention.

tion. At this point *secondary prevention* is your next road to take. The purpose of secondary prevention is to prevent the further deterioration of disease and to help you regain as much functioning as possible and improve upon the quality of your life. This road includes the following activities:

1. Rapid response diagnosis and treatment of your disease
2. Education regarding how to control the disease or its symptoms through *self care*, that is, by your own efforts
3. Lifestyle changes to minimize the expected effects of the disease
4. A case management program to monitor your progress and assist you in receiving the treatment services you need in a timely manner

Sometimes called *tertiary prevention*, the third road is taken when the disease has progressed to a stage where you are seriously ill. Down this road you find activities designed to:

1. Minimize the effects of your disease on other organs or body systems
2. Assist you in adjusting your lifestyle to the limitations presented by the disease
3. Educate you regarding the disease process and how to minimize its effects in your life
4. Provide rapid response medical or surgical treatment of acute episodes
5. Maintain your comfort and minimize your pain if your illness is incurable

Richard Hart, M.D., D.PH., dean of the Loma Linda University School of Public Health, says that measuring the effects of offering health promotion services within managed care is one of the most difficult problems to solve. Several research studies have shown that it takes up to five years or more to reap the results of intense primary prevention services. Because health plan members change health plans every two or three years, the incentive for a health plan to manage health promotion is lost if another health plan reaps the results.

Health plans have succeeded in fulfilling the basic level of health promotion by giving information to members. Some health plans are even experimenting by providing members with health assessments such as blood pressure screening, cholesterol screening, Pap smears, and mammograms. But some health plans are not yet fully committed to providing these higher-cost intervention services designed to encourage health plan members to change their lifestyles in a healthy, permanent way.

HEALTH PROMOTION PROGRAMS
AT HMOs

Here is a list of the more common health promotion programs available at HMOs. It is divided into two large categories, education services and clinical services. In reality, though, it is difficult to artificially separate these two since many clinical services include a strong educational component. Do not expect that your health plan will have *all* of these programs, and don't be fooled by advertising that promises health promotion services. Investigate what specific preventive services are actually available. Use Figure 7-2 as a checklist for yourself.

When was the last time you participated in the following prevention services:

Date	Service
_____	Smoking cessation program
_____	Stress management program
_____	Blood pressure monitoring
_____	Cholesterol screening
_____	Blood sugar level screening
_____	Hearing test
_____	Vision test
_____	Glaucoma test
_____	Weight management
_____	Pharmacy education
_____	Personal exercise program
_____	Nutrition education

FOR WOMEN

Date	Service
_____	Pap test
_____	Breast self examination
_____	Breast examination by a physician or mammogram
_____	Colon-rectal cancer screening

FOR MEN

Date	Service
_____	Prostate screening (for men of certain age)
_____	Testicular self examination
_____	Colon-rectal cancer screening

FIGURE 7-2   Checklist of prevention services.

Education Services

Here are some of the popular classes and services that may be offered by your
health plan:

1. Smoking cessation: recommended for any cigarette smoker.
2. Stress management: recommended for anyone experiencing anxiety, hypertension, or who is at risk of coronary artery disease.
3. Prenatal education: recommended and sometimes required for every pregnant female HMO member.
4. Weight management: recommended for anyone at risk of developing hypertension or diabetes.
5. Breast self-examination: recommended monthly for all women age 18 and over.
6. Nutrition education/counseling: recommended for all pregnant females, older adults, infants and children, or for those at increased risk of various chronic diseases.
7. Personal exercise program: recommended for anyone unless your physician advises otherwise.
8. Testicular self-examination: recommended monthly for all men over the age of 18.
9. Medical history: required at the time of physical exam, at the first visit to your primary care physician, at the onset of any acute injury or illness, and before surgery. This involves filling out a questionnaire telling the physician about the diseases you and your family members have had in the past.
10. Child safety/well-baby care: information recommended or required for the parents of all newborn babies.
11. Self-help groups on a variety of topics: Recommended for anyone with the desire to learn more about self care, health improvement, and disease prevention.
12. Pharmacy education/counseling: recommended for anyone taking medication, and especially recommended for anyone receiving multiple medications.
13. Self care for minor medical problems: recommended for everyone.
14. Diabetes education: recommended or required for anyone diagnosed with diabetes mellitus.
15. Asthma education: recommended or required for anyone diagnosed with asthma.
16. Cardiac rehabilitation: recommended for anyone diagnosed with coronary artery disease.
17. Self care for chronic diseases: recommended for anyone diagnosed with a chronic disease.

18. Social services, such as case management: recommended or required for anyone diagnosed with a serious disease or high-risk medical condition.
19. Post stroke education/rehabilitation: recommended or required for anyone who has been diagnosed with a stroke.
20. Post cardiac surgery rehabilitation: recommended or required for anyone who has had open heart surgery.
21. Pain management programs: recommended for anyone suffering from chronic pain.

Clinical Services

Clinical screening services are designed to tell your managed care team whether you have a disease in its early stages. The idea is that if you can identify the disease early enough you can treat it faster and minimize its negative effects. Physicians debate the effectiveness of some clinical services used as tools for primary prevention. Several things influence how your health plan decides whether a certain test offers enough benefit to you to offset the costs:

1. The average number of false positive results (i.e., test results that show that the disease is present when it is not)
2. The average number of false negative results (i.e., test results that show that the disease is not present when it is)
3. The severity of consequences of accepting false positive and false negative results
4. The likelihood of positive outcomes if disease is detected early
5. The risks of unwanted complications developing as a result of performing the screening procedure
6. The cost of performing the screening procedures

Check with your health plan for any screening procedure you are interested in receiving. Their recommendations may be slightly different from those presented in this book. Here are some of the more commonly used screening services:

1. Cervical cancer screening: Pap smears are recommended every one to three years for all women over the age of 20 or starting after the first intercourse, or yearly for women with multiple sexual partners or those who had an early onset of sexual activity.
2. Prostate cancer screening: Annual digital rectal exam by a physician is recommended for all men over the age of 50, for African-American men over the age of 40, and for men over the age of 40 who have a primary relative diagnosed with prostate cancer.

3. Breast cancer screening: Annual breast exam by a physician is recommended for all women over age 40; annual mammograms are recommended for all women over the age of 50 and every one or two years for women over age 35 to 40 who have had a primary relative diagnosed with breast cancer.

4. Heart disease/cholesterol screening: recommended every five years after the age of 30 or more frequently if other risk factors are present.

5. Blood pressure monitoring: recommended at every visit to the physician or every one to two years, or more frequently if high blood pressure has been diagnosed.

6. Colon-rectal cancer screening: stool laboratory test for occult blood count recommended annually for those over age 50; stool test recommended annually for those over age 40 with a relative diagnosed with colon cancer or with a history of inflammatory bowel disease.

7. Prenatal medical care: recommended or required for pregnant females during the first trimester of pregnancy.

8. Other screening services including cardiac stress test, osteoporosis (bone density) screening, routine physical examination, resting electrocardiogram (EKG), fasting blood sugar test, hematocrit, urinalysis, thyroid testing, and eye sight and hearing exams. If your health plan identifies you as having risk factors for one or more diseases, it pays to listen to the advice given you. If you are in a high-risk category and refuse to comply with certain prevention services, such as case management, you may be at risk of being disenrolled from the plan. Check your benefit agreement or ask your primary care physician for more information.

9. Chronic diseases case management: recommended or required for anyone diagnosed with a chronic disease.

10. Chemical dependency rehabilitation programs: recommended or required for anyone diagnosed with a chemical dependency.

11. Pain management program: recommended for anyone suffering from chronic pain.

NONTRADITIONAL AND EXPERIMENTAL SERVICES

A few managed care organizations are experimenting with nontraditional therapies to promote wellness for HMO members. It is uncertain how popular these services will become in the future. Chiropractic care is offered with some benefit packages. Some health plans are experimenting with acupuncture. Check with your health plan to determine which of these health services are available.

Post-surgical wound care centers specializing in rapid healing are being used in some areas. Most managed care organizations are constantly looking for innovative settings in which care can be provided that results in higher quality and lower costs. A few years ago home care was considered an alternative delivery service. Now it is so commonly used for managed care that it is not an alternative—it is mandatory. In the next few years we will see more experiments with new ways to promote good health and prevent disease.

If you are interested in unconventional therapy as a supplement to traditional medical care, consider the following:

First, talk with your physician about your interests. Recognize that your physician may have a different opinion than you do regarding the effectiveness of unconventional treatments. Then check your health plan benefits; many health plans do not pay for unconventional therapy.

CHAPTER 8

Understanding the Authorization Process

Long-time subscribers of managed care health plans are used to it. Managed care physicians have adjusted their practice styles to accommodate it. However, depending on the health plan as a new subscriber you may not expect it. I'm referring to the *authorization process* in managed care.

Under traditional health insurance programs there is little structure to the relationship between you and the health plan. If you want to see a specialist and the specialist is willing to provide care for you, no authorization is needed. If you want a special procedure and your physician is willing to write a prescription for the service to be performed, no one else needs to be involved in the decision. The situation is different in managed care.

Managed care is a structured relationship between physician, subscriber, and health plan. Things are done more formally. Records are kept on both the medical and the administrative events that occur. Authorization is part of that structure.

If you understand the how and why of authorization, you will not be surprised when it occurs. You will also be prepared to work with your physician and the authorization process to get the most benefit out of it. Why not work with the system to get the best care you can?

WHY AUTHORIZATION IS REQUIRED

Authorization is not needed for primary care services. When you need to see your primary care physician, you schedule a visit. If you need care that your primary care physician cannot provide for you, your physician may need to get authorization to make the referral. The exception to this is when you are in a health plan that gives your physician the power to authorize treatment. Here are ten reasons why the authorization process is used:

1. Verification of eligibility. The first step in authorization is to verify your current membership status in the health plan. There are a couple of reasons for eligibility verification. First, verifying eligibility assists the provider in determining which plan you are enrolled in. Second, in the more integrated delivery systems, this verification process can confirm for the provider what financial obligations, if any, you may have to fulfill at the time you receive services. Third, managed care organizations want to prevent fraudulent use of the benefits that are offered to subscribers.

2. Certification that the benefit agreement is followed. The authorization process makes sure that you get what you deserve while the health plan does not pay for services that you are not entitled to receive.

3. Paying claims to contracted providers. This is not usually an issue in staff model HMOs since the physicians all work for the health plan. However, in network model HMOs and IPA model HMOs, this is an important issue. Authorization starts a computerized record that is used to pay the provider after you receive the authorized service. In most organizations, if a specialist asks the health plan to pay for services he or she performed for you, the specialist will not receive payment unless there is a formal record of authorization.

4. Validating the medical necessity and appropriateness of care. You always have available to you through the authorization process professionals who can advise you and your primary care physician whether the recommended care is appropriate, protecting you from receiving treatment that could be harmful.

5. Screening for procedures that require a second opinion. Certain medical and surgical procedures are high risk. When any of these procedures are being considered, the authorization process will automatically remind your physician that a second surgical opinion is required before proceeding. You should ask for second opinions on your own, but if you don't, the managed care authorization process has a built-in method for requesting them.

6. Screening for medications that fall outside of the formulary (the list of prescription medications that have been accepted for use by the managed care organization, as discussed in Chapter 5). If your physician believes that you need a medicine that is not on this list, he or she will obtain authorization for that medicine. During the authorization process the physician will receive information from a pharmacist or other physicians regarding alternate medicines that may be just as effective.

7. Screening for the appropriate setting in which the service is to be provided. The acute care hospital is no longer the center for delivering health care. Skilled nursing facilities, home nursing services, and free-standing surgery centers are being used more frequently. This assures the health plan that patients are sent to preferred or contracted providers.

8. Providing information for case management. The authorization process assists your physician in identifying when *case management* is appropriate. Case management, discussed in Chapter 11, is a process of assisting the health plan member in getting needed care at the most appropriate time. Not only are the details of your situation quickly relayed to your case manager, but the other members of your care team are notified as well.

9. Tracking utilization patterns. The authorization process creates the opportunity to gather a lot of information about physicians. The health plan medical director will be able to monitor which physicians follow health plan referral policies closely, which physicians get the best results, and which physicians either overuse or underuse services.

10. Controlling costs and financial management. Through minimizing referral to inappropriate services, the authorization process reduces the cost of providing care. For example, if you are admitted to a hospital a whole day before a scheduled surgery, the health plan would be paying for care that is not necessary. Authorizations also alert financial managers regarding the amount of money that should be set aside for claims expected in the future. If surgery is authorized this month, the surgeon will submit a claim next month and should be paid within thirty days.

WHO AUTHORIZES?

Depending on your health plan and its internal structure you may have more than one person or group that participates in the authorization process. In some health plans, such as with the Group Health Cooperative of Puget Sound in Seattle, any physician is empowered to authorize services without involving other people. Dr. Al Truscott, medical director of Group Health Cooperative, explains that

> it is not just the primary care physicians who give authorization. We have 400 specialists who are employed by us who make the more expensive decisions and they are equally independent or autonomous in their decisions. That is not to say that there are times when we have chosen to make a health plan-wide decision about how things will be accomplished. But when this happens the physicians collaborate together in such a decision.

In cases of complicated procedures or very high-cost procedures such as organ transplants, however, other levels of discussion might take place, since sending a patient for these services may involve going outside the system to another organization.

In a few cases you, as the subscriber, may have to contact the authorization department to inform them that you expect to use a certain health care service. When you make this type of call, you usually will speak to a utilization review nurse who will check your eligibility and verify the benefit agreement details. Then you will receive information about where the services should be performed.

Many health plans have a utilization management committee or authorization review committee. The task of this committee is to consider and act upon all the requests for authorization that are presented by physicians. Comprised of a multidisciplinary team of medical professionals, the committee meets on a regularly scheduled basis. Highly organized and experienced authorization teams make the process of seeking an authorization seem almost effortless. Disorganized or less experienced teams can result in frustration and anger for both you and your physician.

Keeping track of authorizations is everyone's responsibility. Health plan managers, medical directors, primary care physicians, specialists, and HMO facilities all keep records of what services are authorized. As the primary consumer of managed care you, too, should be aware when an authorization is given.

AUTOMATIC AUTHORIZATIONS

In most health plans some services not available from your primary care physician are automatically authorized. Here is a list of procedures that are often automatically approved:

1. Pap smears
2. Simple X-rays
3. Vaccinations
4. Breast biopsies
5. Hernia repair
6. Mammograms
7. Certain lab tests
8. Referrals to case management
9. Referrals to a specialist for specific conditions and for an initial consultation only

WHAT NEEDS TO BE AUTHORIZED

In general, anything that your primary care physician cannot do in the office will need an authorization. Here is a list of the more common services for which an authorization request will be needed:

1. Admission to the hospital
2. Care in the emergency room

3. Continued stay in the hospital
4. Transfer to another facility
5. Access to alternative care settings
6. Experimental procedures
7. CT scan and MRI diagnostic procedures
8. Nuclear diagnostic procedures
9. Treadmill stress tests
10. Invasive diagnostic and therapeutic procedures
11. Inpatient surgery
12. Same day surgery
13. Any high-cost service

Your health plan should inform you regarding which services need prior authorization before receiving them. If you do not receive this information, ask your physician about it.

In some health plans, if you miss an appointment for an authorized service or if you wait too long before making the appointment once it has been authorized, you may need to have the service authorized again. Seem unfair? Look at it this way: If you miss an appointment without having informed your physician ahead of time, how is he or she to interpret this? It cannot be assumed that you are interested in receiving the service unless you actually show up to receive it. Also, if you miss the appointment, the health plan cannot assume that you are still eligible for services after that date. If you are unwilling or unable to receive a service, your physician needs to know this.

RESULTS OF AUTHORIZATIONS

After your physician submits the request for authorization, it will either be approved, delayed, or denied. Most often, your requests will be approved. Delays can occur in the authorization process when more information is needed before a decision can be made. Denied authorizations usually come back to your physician with an explanation of why the denial was given along with a statement of what alternatives are recommended.

Authorization for emergency treatment should be given immediately if you have a true medical emergency (see Chapter 15). The best health plans and medical groups are able to process the majority of requests for authorizations within 24 hours. You or your physician should have to wait no more than one week for an authorization. Figure 8-1 lists seven characteristics of the best authorization programs, and Figure 8-2 lists important steps to follow to assure that your authorization process runs smoothly.

The best authorization programs:

1. Are open to dialogue with your physician
2. Attempt to customize care to your needs
3. Give your primary care physician more authority to approve requests
4. Respond to authorization requests quickly to minimize delays in your care
5. Have a variety of providers from which to choose for referrals
6. Have information systems that manage the process
7. Have primary care physicians participate in the authorization process

---

FIGURE 8-1   Seven characteristics of the best authorization programs.

---

1. Don't wait to make your request to the primary care physician for special services. The longer you wait the more the process will be delayed.
2. Keep your appointments for authorized services. If you have to miss an appointment, inform your physician as far in advance as possible.
3. If you do not want the service that is about to be authorized, discuss this with your physician before the authorization process begins.
4. Ask what procedures and services automatically require a second opinion in your health plan.
5. If you have a question about where a specific service will be performed, discuss this with your physician.
6. Ask your health plan how long it takes to get authorizations approved.
7. If you or your physician receives an authorization for a service, identify the specific details, such as:
   a. the specific service
   b. the number of times the service is authorized to be performed
   c. whether additional services are expected and when authorization should be obtained for these
   d. which provider is specified
   e. the time limit within which the service must be received
   f. the expected outcome from the service
   g. any special instructions
8. If your authorization request is denied, make sure you understand the explanation. Discuss with your physician the alternatives available to you.
9. If you do not get a response to your authorization request during the time that you expected, ask for an explanation for the delay.

FIGURE 8-2   Steps toward a smooth authorization process.

CHAPTER 9

Going to the Managed Care Hospital

Under managed care the need for hospitals is changing. Fewer people go to the hospital under managed care plans compared with traditional insurance plans. A fifteen-year trend shows that admissions to hospitals have declined 25 percent and that the average length of time spent in the hospital has declined almost 30 percent. When health plan members go to the hospital it is usually for outpatient services. In fact, a fifteen-year trend shows that the average number of outpatient visits made each year has increased almost 50 percent. Hospitals are remaking themselves into outpatient facilities with some inpatient beds available for patients who are too sick to remain outside the hospital.

There are only a few ways you will be admitted to the hospital if you are a managed care member. If you go to the hospital emergency room, the ER physician or nurse will evaluate your situation and call either your primary care physician or the health plan medical director to discuss your case. If it is determined that you have a medical emergency, you will be treated and stabilized until you are well enough to return home or go to another treatment center to receive care. Your health plan will be notified of your admission to the hospital.

You could also be admitted to the hospital for an elective procedure that is not otherwise available in another facility in the community. Your physician will either authorize your visit to the hospital or will see that authorization is obtained from the health plan or the medical group prior to scheduling your stay there.

HOW YOUR CARE TEAM KNOWS
WHETHER YOU NEED TO BE HOSPITALIZED

You are not expected to know all the details of your condition. However, if you understand the concepts that your managed care team is concerned about, you are more likely to be an active participant in the care decisions that need to be made. Also, if you have a chronic condition that needs to be monitored (whether you are in the hospital or not), you should learn the indicators of your health status that your care team monitors.

So how does your managed care team know whether you are sick enough to be admitted to the hospital? What do they look for that indicates your health status? Your managed care team looks at two broad categories when assessing whether you need to be in the hospital: How severe your illness is and the type of service you need given your current condition. Severity of illness is indicated by a number of factors:

1. **Body temperature.** One vital sign of your health status is your body temperature. Normal body temperature is 98.6 degrees Fahrenheit when using an oral thermometer. A body temperature above 102 degrees can be severe and may indicate a need for hospitalization if other conditions are also present such as an infection. Your primary care physician is the one to make this determination.
2. **Pulse.** A sustained low pulse rate of 40 beats per minute or less is dangerous. This indicator in itself may be enough to send you to the hospital for care. On the high end, a sustained pulse rate of 140 beats per minute is an indicator of a problem that needs the medical attention available at a hospital.
3. **Respiration.** Individuals with a chronic pulmonary disease may have a respiration rate that is higher than normal on a continuing basis. A rate above 28 respirations per minute can be considered dangerous. If this situation occurs, your physician should evaluate your condition.
4. **Blood pressure.** You probably know that blood pressure usually has two numbers associated with it: systolic and diastolic. If the systolic pressure is either too low or too high, it may indicate a need for hospitalization. Or if the diastolic pressure is too high, you may need to be in the hospital. The normal range is 120 to 130 over 70 to 80.
5. **Blood test results.** The blood is an amazing signal device for your managed care team. Many common tests can be performed that measure such elements as hemoglobin, hematocrit, white blood cells, sodium, potassium, oxygen, carbon dioxide, bacteria, and toxic chemical substances. When the lab test results show abnormal high or low values, you may need to be in the hospital. Blood tests are often used in connection with monitoring other indicators of health status. If certain blood tests are routinely performed for your condition, learn what they are and what they mean.
6. **Functional impairment.** Here are some examples of functional impairments that could send you to the hospital:
   a. you suddenly lose your balance and are unable to regain it
   b. you are found unconscious

    c. you have extreme weakness

    d. you suddenly lose the function of any body part

    e. you are in severe pain

7. Other physical problems. Severe uncontrolled bleeding is a life-threatening problem and should be cared for at a hospital. Hospitalization may be required if you have a foreign body in an airway or your intestinal track. Severe vomiting or diarrhea may be an indicator of the need for hospital care.

Another reason for needing hospital care is if you have a condition that requires high-intensity service not available at the physician's office. Intensity includes the complexity of the service, how often it must be performed, how dangerous it is, and how many health care professionals need to be involved. The most common types of high-intensity services include the need to frequently monitor your vital signs, administer fluids and medications under nursing supervision, and receive treatments or procedures too dangerous to be performed outside the hospital.

The decision to be admitted to the hospital is a simple one if your heart stops beating or you are unconscious. At other times it is a complex decision that can be made only after performing several tests and using a technique developed by managed care teams called the "23-hour admission." A 23-hour admission is when you are taken to the hospital for an observation period of no more than 23 hours. During this observation period tests are performed and your managed care team makes the decision whether you need to remain in the hospital.

HOSPITAL NURSING CARE

You may go to the hospital for a surgical procedure, but one of the main reasons you stay in the hospital is the need for nursing care during your recovery. For the majority of patients it is this round-the-clock nursing care that makes the hospital what it is.

Nurses approach their work systematically. As a patient you are taken through a continuous nursing process where your condition is evaluated, a decision is made regarding your current health status and what type of nursing care is needed, a nursing plan is created and implemented, and then your condition is evaluated again to determine how effective the nursing care has been. This process is repeated as many times as is necessary until you can leave the hospital.

Nurses coordinate every aspect of your hospital care. For many common conditions requiring hospitalization, nurses have developed *care maps* or *critical paths* which guide their work. For example, if you have a knee joint replaced the nursing care map sets reasonable objectives for improvement of your knee for each day of hospital care. Every patient presents different needs, yet there are a lot of common needs that patients have with the same condition. The care map is an attempt by your nursing care team to provide an individualized program of care based upon the best nursing practices known.

It is important to remain an active participant in the process of care while you are in the hospital. Discuss your situation with your hospital nurses and your physician. Give them your opinions regarding treatment procedures and your progress. This active approach will assist you in maintaining as much control as possible during hospitalization.

Why Doesn't the Nurse Come When I Ring My Bell?

This is a question that has been asked since the invention of the hospital bedside call button: You are in the same room with a patient who has the same diagnosis. You watch the nurse come in and out and you wonder why the other patient gets more attention than you get. There are many reasons (and one is not because the nurse likes that patient better). Some patients just need more care than do others. Here's why.

Nursing care is given based on how acutely ill each patient is. Nurse managers call it *acuity,* or the level of intensity with which nursing care must be provided (see Figure 9-1). Acuity is influenced by many factors, but here are a few of the most common ones:

High acuity = Complex care
              Frequent need for personal attention
              Higher barriers to care
              Greater severity of illness
              Unstable vital signs
              Self-care needs are greater
              Emotional coping deficit present

Low acuity = Simple care
             Infrequent need for personal attention
             Barriers to care are lower
             Stable vital signs
             Lower severity of illness
             Self-care needs are fewer
             Emotional need for reassurance

FIGURE 9-1   Levels of acuity.

1. Body fluid imbalances may require intravenous care and constant monitoring.
2. Some surgical wounds are simple; others are complex. The possibility of infection increases the acuity even more.
3. Some medications must be given continuously and others can be given just a few times each day.
4. If you must be kept in an isolation room, the acuity level goes up.
5. If you have just returned from surgery your vital signs will need frequent monitoring. But if you are almost ready to go home, vital signs are monitored less frequently.
6. Some patients may need assistance with the simplest of activities while others can care for themselves without the aid of a nurse.
7. If you have a hearing, sight, speech, or language barrier, acuity goes up because it simply takes more time to discuss your care with you.
8. Nurses must check drainage devices and tubes frequently to make sure they are cared for appropriately.

So, if your nurse can't get to you immediately, it could be that your condition has improved and that higher priority is being given to patients with more urgent needs. If you are curious about your acuity level, ask the nurse to tell you about it.

Figure 9-2 describes what you can do while in the hospital to be an active participant in your care.

---

1. Bring to the hospital your health plan ID card and information about your physician or medical group to which you have been assigned. Having your physician's name, address, and phone number available at the outset will minimize confusion.
2. If you kept a list of symptoms that you presented to your physician, bring it to the hospital to show the nurses.
3. If you know you are going to be admitted to the hospital or if you have to go to the emergency room, leave valuable jewelry, credit cards, and cash at home.
4. If you regularly take medications, discuss this with your physician before going to the hospital.
5. Don't try to be a hero by hiding your symptoms. Be open with your nursing care team. Give them your opinions regarding the procedures and tests prescribed for you.
6. Participate in the care mapping process by asking questions and reviewing your progress according to the care map. If you don't seem to be achieving the objectives, discuss this with your physician.
7. If you are hearing- or speech-impaired and need another person or special equipment to assist you in communicating with your managed care team, tell your physician.

FIGURE 9-2   How to be an active participant in your hospital care.

CHAPTER 10

Understanding Utilization Management

When you are healthy it is difficult to imagine going to the physician, having all kinds of tests performed, and engaging the services of the best specialists. But once you get an unexplained illness or uncomfortable symptoms, your attitude can change dramatically. Now you will stop at nothing to get relief: Call in the best physicians. Have the most thorough diagnostic procedures performed. Get extra tests done if needed, just to be sure. Never mind how much it costs.

Left unchecked the national appetite for medical services is almost insatiable. The more services are available, the more they are used as long as there is someone to pay the bill. And, when someone else pays the bill, both the patient and physician have little concern for how much the health care system is used as long as the best services are available.

UTILIZATION MANAGEMENT IS NOT NEW

For many years hospital medical staff organizations used a process known as *utilization review,* or UR, to retrospectively (after you were discharged) evaluate the appropriateness of hospital care. This meant that after you were discharged utilization review committees evaluated your medical record, or "charts," to determine whether hospital services were used in an effective manner.

Then, in the early 1980s, hospitals realized that the federal government would start paying for Medicare patients on a "dollar amount per diagnosis" basis (that is, payment would be on the basis of the patient's diagnosis, rather than the hospital's account of services rendered). For the first time hospitals felt an internal pressure to wisely manage health care resources since their financial survival depended upon it. Utilization review committees immediately started to expand their work. Now a whole range of utilization review activities are used.

WHAT UTILIZATION MANAGEMENT INCLUDES

Sometimes health care is overused. Sometimes it is underused (see Figures 10-1 and 10-2). The goal of utilization management is to reduce both overuse and underuse of services. To achieve this, utilization reviewers use the following management tools:

1. **Medical necessity review.** If you are sent to the hospital by your physician, you may be evaluated for 23 hours or less to determine if there is a *medi-*

Health plans are always on the watch for indicators of overutilization. Here are some of things they watch for:

1. Discharge planning is not complete when you are ready for discharge.
2. Medical equipment is not ready when you are.
3. Diagnostic tests may be duplicated if you change physicians.
4. A mistake is made during a procedure.
5. The prescribed treatment is not effective.
6. You have another illness that was not known about.
7. You get complications as a result of services performed.
8. An error is made in the type of treatment prescribed.
9. You have the procedure performed as an inpatient when you could have had it as an outpatient.
10. Services are ordered on a "rush" basis.
11. You wait too long before seeking care.
12. You go physician shopping.
13. A high-cost procedure is used when a low-cost procedure would have given the same results.
14. You do not comply with your physician's advice.
15. You do not show up for your appointment.
16. You have unnecessary surgery performed.
17. You are treated by a professional who lacks experience.
18. You went to the hospital emergency room when you could have gone to a primary care physician's office.
19. The physician wants to take extra precautions because he or she is fearful of a malpractice lawsuit.
20. Members of your managed care team do not communicate with one another regarding your condition and your needs.
21. Your physician refers you to a specialist and gives this consultant carte blanche to do what ever he or she desires.
22. Your health plan has liberal benefits.
23. Medical suppliers increase their prices.
24. You get injured in an accident.

FIGURE 10-1   Fifty causes of overuse of services.

cal necessity for admission. If during this time your physician and nurses identify that you do meet the criteria for admission, you will be assigned a bed. Once you are admitted to the hospital the UR staff continues to monitor medical necessity every step along the way, including procedures to be used and extra days needed for your hospital stay.

2. Precertification or prior authorization. An activity closely related to the medical necessity of admission is obtaining precertification or authorization.

---

25. You engage in a behavior that is known to increase your risk of getting sick or injured.
26. The medical instruments used to perform procedures are not properly calibrated.
27. A diagnostic test gives a false positive result.
28. You are admitted to the hospital when you could have been cared for at home or in the physician's office.
29. You were sent to a subspecialist for care when you could have been treated by a primary care physician.
30. You develop a chronic condition.
31. Your managed care team does not know which treatment will give the best results.
32. Your care team gets confused about what should be done.
33. You are confused about what your physician expects of you.
34. You demand services that are inappropriate.
35. The hospital is out of stock for a product that you need.
36. Your HMO uses a provider that is not under a contract that offers better prices than "usual and customary."
37. You get better but no one notices this at first.
38. You get worse but no one notices this at first.
39. You are provided services that are not covered by your health plan.
40. You lack knowledge of how to manage your illness yourself.
41. You have to be readmitted to the hospital soon after discharge.
42. You are not informed regarding your treatment alternatives and your condition gets worse.
43. You do not have a strong social support system for independent living.
44. Utilization management is only partially used or not used at all.
45. There is a wide variety in physician's practice patterns for the same medical conditions.
46. Language barriers make communication slower.
47. Your condition makes it more difficult to learn the self-care skills you need for going home.
48. The operating room schedule is too full.
49. You or your family delays a medical decision.
50. Someone forgets to order a test.

FIGURE 10-1   *(Continued)*

Health plans realize that sometimes underutilization can turn into overutilization if they are not careful. Yet sometimes you get well in spite of using fewer resources or less costly resources than the average person. Here are twelve causes of underutilization.

1. Your physician is incorrect in his or her diagnosis.
2. Your condition is less severe than expected and you get well sooner than expected.
3. You are discharged before you are ready to leave the hospital.
4. Utilization management is only partially used or not used at all.
5. You (or your physician) settle for a treatment option that is second best, but you get well anyway.
6. A new, effective medical treatment is developed that avoids the usual pattern of utilization.
7. Your health plan's authorization criteria are too strict.
8. You do not understand all your options.
9. Your medical director is inflexible.
10. Your physician or medical director has expectations that are too high regarding your ability to get well.
11. Your primary care physician does not refer you to a specialist for care when you should be referred.
12. You have a higher tolerance than most other members for pain and discomfort.

FIGURE 10-2   Twelve causes of underuse of services.

3. Length of stay review. Before you are admitted, a utilization reviewer makes an initial judgment regarding how many days you should be in the hospital based upon your medical condition. This is known as a *length of stay review*. Then during your stay at the hospital reviewers compare how long you are staying compared with other patients with similar conditions.

4. Concurrent review. *Concurrent review* is conducted of the timeliness of diagnostic and therapeutic services. For example, UR nurses monitor whether X rays are taken in a timely manner and, if not, why. Concurrent review often extends to other issues such as the quality of care, severity of illness, intensity of treatments given and the level of care you receive.

5. Peer review. If you experience a negative result of being in the hospital (for example, an unexpected problem occurs, such as an infection or injury), your medical record will be evaluated to determine why this occurred. Since it is your physician who is in charge of managing your care while you are in the hospital, his or her clinical judgment and actions are subject to *peer review* during this process.

6. Grievance review. If something serious happens and you or your family members file a formal grievance, the utilization review committee will

automatically evaluate it. This *grievance review* will include your medical records and records and logs from other departments documenting what occurred, when it occurred, what was done about it at the time, who was notified, and so forth.

7. Same-day surgery. Sometimes called short-stay surgery or outpatient surgery, *same-day surgery* allows you to go home the same day that the surgery is performed. Rapidly becoming the most common form of surgery, same-day surgery cannot be performed for every type of surgery but only those where it is safe for you to go home within a few hours after the procedure.

8. Retrospective review. After you are discharged from the hospital reviewers conduct a *retrospective review* in which they look back in your medical records to identify areas where care could have been improved. Knowing your health status at the time of discharge, the utilization review staff try to find any specific events or parts of the process of your care that raised cost or lowered quality.

9. Alternative care selection. Whenever your health plan can find an alternative to acute care that provides the level of care you need at a lower cost, it will attempt to do so. Alternatives to acute care include skilled nursing facilities, step down units, rehabilitation facilities, home care, and hospice care.

10. Member education. Health education regarding how to control your own health status and promote wellness is one way to improve the quality of life of HMO members. HMOs have found that when they educate members regarding their options, they are more satisfied with their care.

11. Contracting policies. HMOs try to contract with a few high-quality providers of care to maintain formal communications and closely monitor the quality of care you receive.

12. Critical paths. Because of the frequency with which your hospital managed care team deals with certain medical conditions, they have been able to outline on paper the course of treatment that has been shown in the past to have the best results for quick recovery. *Critical paths* act as checkpoints to monitor whether your condition is improving as desired.

13. Medical practice guidelines. Designed primarily for physicians, *medical practice guidelines* are written outlines of protocols to follow in treating specific diseases. Guidelines cover both diagnostic procedures and treatment plans.

14. Case management. Once you are selected for *case management,* a case manager monitors your health status and assists you in getting the care you need to keep you as healthy as possible.

15. Continuing care planning. Known for many years as "discharge planning," *continuing care planning* involves someone (often a case manager)

who assists you in making the transition from inpatient hospital care to either your home or to some other appropriate place for care.

16. Computer reports. The heart of managed care is utilization management and the heart of utilization management is information about quality and costs. Most HMOs gather detailed information on what services are used, how often they are used, what types of patients use them, and what these services cost the health plan, as indicators of quality. They use computers to help them analyze this data.

17. Staff training. Health plans and their contracted providers spend thousands of dollars constantly training patient care staff in the techniques and systems that produce the best outcomes. Health care organizations find that bringing in outside temporary employees who do not understand the systems costs them more in the short and long run. A higher and higher priority is given to creating a unified workforce that is familiar with the inner workings of the organization. So, many of these organizations are cross-training their employees to be able to perform more than one function. The old maxim still holds true today: the better the nursing care, the sooner the patient will recover.

18. Logistics improvement. Cooperation between nursing personnel and other health care professionals is the key to effective health care. Here are some of the ways that logistics influence utilization management:
    a. Improved hospital support services, such as housekeeping and engineering, minimize breakdowns and delays.
    b. Formal methods for resolving disagreements and clarifying expectations smooth the interpersonal dynamics of health care and create efficiencies.
    c. Problems that arise repeatedly are reported, and clear responsibilities are delegated to prevent problems from continuing.

BE INVOLVED IN THE UTILIZATION MANAGEMENT PROCESS

Dr. Cary Sennett, previously Medical Staff Director for Clinical Planning and Improvement at Group Health Cooperative of Puget Sound in Seattle, says that to most appropriately interact with the utilization management process

> you should be actively involved in decisions about your care. You should discuss your situation with your physician. Utilization management will work best in the long run when information flows to you through the physician who can communicate the rationale for utilization management protocols. In some settings this may not be working

as it should. So, what I recommend is that you challenge the system. Be eager to be involved in decisions about your care. In the last analysis utilization management shouldn't be a set of protocols that is superimposed on physician care. There can't be a screen through which care filters, through which decisions filter. Ideally, utilization management should be a set of decision support technologies made available to the physician to help the physican and patient make the decision most appropriate for that patient.

Use Figure 10-3 as a checklist of what to expect from your utilization management department and what you can do to play your part in utilization management.

---

1. Accessibility. Every health plan and medical group is different regarding accessibility. Find out what the local practice is. If there is no telephone line for members to use, what other means does the utilization management department use to create accessibility?
2. Responsiveness. In health care, timing sometimes means the difference between comfort and discomfort, health and illness, and even life and death. How quickly does the utilization management department respond to your physician's request for authorization?
3. Make sure that you understand what your health plan expects of you. Read the orientation materials you receive.
4. Get information on your condition. If you ask for a detailed explanation of your situation, you should be able to get it. If you do not receive it promptly, persist in your request until you do get the information.
5. Ask to speak with the UR nurse. This individual will be able to give you a lot of valuable information about your care.
6. Give your UR nurse feedback on the quality of care you receive from all outside organizations.
7. Ask to see the critical path for your medical condition. This will give you a good idea what to expect in the few days ahead.
8. If you feel uncomfortable about the recommended treatment option, talk to your physician. If you think that you need a higher level of care than is recommended, ask for an explanation of the clinical criteria that were used for your case.

FIGURE 10-3 What to expect from and how to play your part in utilization management.

CHAPTER 11

Managing High Risk through Case Management

John, a 67-year-old retired auto worker, has diabetes. For many years John controlled his disease but lately he has had repeated bouts with his blood sugar getting out of control. In the last nine months John was hospitalized twice. Before John was discharged from the hospital the second time, he was assigned to a community case manager. By telephone, his case manager followed John and his wife home from the hospital, and then visited them in their home. John's case manager now makes regular contact with John and his wife to determine to what degree John is following the doctor's medical advice. Since John had a difficult time remembering everything he learned when he was in the hospital, the case manager reinforces the information John needs to keep his blood sugar under control and stay out of the hospital.

John is just one example of an HMO member who benefits from case management. Without case managers working for them, John and others like him might have difficulty obtaining the services they need to maintain their health.

WHICH HMO MEMBERS ARE ELIGIBLE FOR CASE MANAGEMENT?

Comprehensive case management like John receives would be too expensive to provide for every HMO member whether or not they are ill. Besides, many health plan members do not need someone like a case manager to assist them in navigating around the system.

Figure 11-1 lists some of the situations where case management is beneficial to you. If you are a managed care plan member already and fall into one of the categories described in Figure 11-1, and a case manager has not been assigned to you yet, your health plan is probably thinking of doing so.

---

1. If you have a chronic illness or other highly complex medical condition, such as diabetes, renal failure, congestive heart failure, chronic obstructive pulmonary disease (COPD), or asthma
2. If you are in a high-risk pregnancy
3. If you exhibit cognitive or developmental deficits
4. If you have emotional problems
5. If you have an inadequate social support system
6. If you have had multiple, concurrent illnesses
7. If you have a history of frequent admissions to the hospital
8. If you use the hospital emergency room frequently
9. If you have a terminal illness
10. If you have a spinal cord injury, amputation, or other trauma

---

FIGURE 11-1   Situations where case management is criticial.

WHY HMOs USE CASE MANAGEMENT

No one in managed care denies that case management can save money in the long run, especially for high-risk patients. Consider these astounding statistics:

■ It has been estimated by various researchers that American business can save at least $20 billion dollars by eliminating the waste of unnecessary care. Case managers assist in this savings.

■ High-risk patients represent only about 5% of the total patient population, yet they are responsible for 70% of the health care expenses.

There are other benefits, too. Without a case manager working with you, you and your family will have a more difficult time making decisions about what care is appropriate. You might not be able to locate services even if you know what to ask for. Your case manager knows that, as a health plan member, you may not be an expert on the complexities of the health system. Loaded with the knowledge that is difficult for you to obtain on your own, your case manager has the time to teach you the details about what types of organizations are available to care for you, what it will be like receiving care from these organizations, and what results to expect. Your case manager will also follow up with you after you receive care to make sure that the care you received was appropriate.

If you are transferred to a skilled nursing facility, your case manager will make contact with the facility to confirm the level of care that you should be receiving. He or she will also confirm with you or your family whether the service you receive is satisfactory.

Case managers can save the HMO money, but they can also save you money, too. Without the guidance of a case manager, your family could easily use up a lifetime of savings in a few months of expensive care. With the case manager's help you can conserve your savings by staying within the maximum spending limits your health plan allows for certain healthcare services. Your case manager understands your benefit agreement better than most people.

Finally, and more importantly, case management can help you achieve the highest quality of life possible given your medical condition. Case management strives to achieve decreased fragmentation of care, increased collaboration from your managed care team, and increased satisfaction for all organizations providing care.

WORKING WITH A CASE MANAGER

Screening and Assessment

If a health plan case manager contacts you or your family it is because your medical condition has already been discussed with your physician or someone else on your managed care team. They will have a general understanding of your condition and may call you on the telephone to discuss your situation. This initial phase of case management is called *screening.*

Alyce Sease, R.N., care coordinator for Kaiser Permanente in Fontana, California, says that in her case management department the case management nurses get involved with the patients even if the patient is not in the hospital:

> If a patient goes to the doctor's office and the doctor thinks that case management will help the patient, the nurse will go right over to the doctor's office to see the patient and begin the process immediately. I get information on every member who is in our hospital. I look at the diagnosis of each inpatient. I look for patients who might be at high risk. But sometimes I get a call from a family member who has heard about our program. And, sometimes the patient will call me directly. They don't necessarily say 'I need a case manager,' but they will explain their situation and we get involved immediately.

Following the initial contact with you, the case manager will complete a formal *assessment* of your situation. This may involve a thorough discussion with you or your family members about a whole range of topics, such as your age and other specifics, your understanding of your situation, your capabilities for caring for yourself, specific needs which make it more difficult carrying out your physician's advice, and the degree of involvement of others in your social support system. Some case managers use written questionnaires during the assessment.

After the assessment is completed, the case manager will collaborate with your physician to determine whether you meet the criteria for case management. The decision will depend to a great degree upon the recommendation that the case manager makes.

Creating a Plan of Action

Your next contact with the case manager may be when you are notified of your acceptance into the program. Then the usual approach is for the case manager to create with you a *plan of action.* In the best case management programs across the country, you or a member of your family is highly involved during the planning step. This is one of the greatest benefits of case management—you get to be involved in making decisions.

Whenever possible, your case manager will look for high-quality services at a reasonable cost to you and to the health plan. Your case manager should be prepared to present to you the available alternatives. For example, your case manager should be prepared to discuss the benefits and availability of home nursing care and rehabilitation programs in your area.

Implementing and Monitoring Your Progress

Your case manager's job has only begun when the planning is complete. Now comes the difficult part of the job: *implementing* the plan and *monitoring* your progress.

If you are being referred to another organization for follow-up care, your case manager will typically provide it with an orientation of your situation before you arrive. Sometimes there is a lot of work involved arranging for the transfer to another organization; case managers will do the leg work necessary to find a service available to do this. If you did this yourself, it could take hours. Sometimes negotiations with the new organization are required if you have special needs.

An important part of your case manager's job is to monitor your progress by evaluating the frequency and intensity with which services are provided. For example, if your program is designed to help you develop personal care skills, your case manager will evaluate how much teaching is going on during the sessions. She will ask questions or observe the program in session to obtain firsthand knowledge of how you are being treated. If the case manager observes major problems or weaknesses in the program, it is her responsibility to report this to the administrator of the program. Your case manager should keep your primary care physician informed on a regular basis, too.

1. Be sure that you communicate clearly what your needs and desires are.
2. Avoid letting your pride get in the way of the benefits of case management. It is not easy to admit that we sometimes need help. If you are in a difficult daily living situation, be honest with your case manager.
3. If you believe that your goals are not being strongly represented during the authorization process, ask your case manager to discuss the situation with you.
4. Remember that if you need services from an organization that has no formal relationship with your medical group or health plan, the authorization process can take a little longer than usual.
5. If you feel uncomfortable about what the case manager suggests, ask "What are the alternatives?"
6. If your case manager seems too busy to adequately give you the information you need, or if unexpected problems occur, talk to your case manager and your primary care physician about it.
7. If you must relocate after getting started with a case manager, be sure to inform your case manager and your physician before you move to avoid confusion and delays.
8. Finally, personality conflicts can arise. If you are assigned to a case manager who is difficult to get along with, ask to be reassigned.

FIGURE 11-2   Guidelines for establishing and maintaining a positive relationship with your case manager.

Periodically your case manager will conduct an assessment to document your progress, creating a document that becomes a permanent part of your medical record. Periodic review of your progress gives your physician an opportunity to make changes in the care you receive.

Figure 11-2 provides a list of guidelines on how to establish and maintain the best possible relationship with your case manager.

CASE MANAGEMENT CAN ACHIEVE DRAMATIC RESULTS

Case management is now commonplace in managed care plans because of dramatic results seen when HMOs began using case management principles on specific types of patients. For example, Mary Hodges, R.N., director of utilization management and case management for Universal Care Health Plan, began using case management for members who had chronic problems with asthma, a condition in which it is very difficult to breathe during the acute stage. She says:

We had 900 cases of asthma in one year where many of the members were constantly going to the hospital. In one month, for example, we had 130 members go to the hospital emergency room for care for asthma attacks. Seventy of these were admitted for at least a two-day stay. So we sent a nurse to every one of those member's homes. We got orders from their physician to teach them how to use special breathing treatment machines all on their own. We trained members on the proper dose of medicine that should be used for treatments. We trained them how to maintain their own breathing machine and keep it clean. When the member started having difficulty breathing the member would know when they could give their own breathing treatment right at home. Within three months of teaching members how to use the machines, we went down from 70 admissions per month to just two per month. And the members love being able to give themselves a treatment that will keep them out of the hospital. The member can catch the problem before it gets out of hand. In just fifteen or twenty minutes after one breathing treatment most asthma patients have their breathing stabilized.

Case management is one of those managed care services that is not highly visible. Not many members know about it. Those who do, love it, because it is rewarding for both you and your case manager when you achieve your health care goals.

CHAPTER   1 2

Practice Guidelines

Here is a little quiz:

Question: Which of the following is the most influential in successfully managing the quality and the cost of your health care?

Answer: (select one)

a. Your hospital utilization managers
b. Your health plan utilization managers
c. Your physician
d. Your health plan administrator

While you ponder this question, consider these hints: The most influential person or organization in the success of managed care knows the most about your care on a day-to-day basis, is legally responsible for access to prescription medicines, and controls how almost 80 percent of the resources are spent for your care. While all three answers are correct to some degree, the best answer is "c," your physician.

Your physician is the most influential person for managing quality and cost. Yet many health care experts say that medical science still does not know enough about what creates the best clinical outcomes in the most cost-effective manner. Mark Zitter, president of The Zitter Group and the Center for Outcomes Information in San Francisco, says

> what we know is that we have tremendous variations in both care and cost and these don't seem to be tied to outcomes. If you look at Medicare data, for example, and look simply for how many dollars Medicare spends per person in different parts of the country, you will find that there is more than a 100% difference between some cities. If the outcomes for both areas are roughly equal, then Medicare is paying too much in some cities. If we are getting better clinical outcomes in the cities where more is spent, then we should look at how they spend their money there and how these resources contribute to better outcomes. But, if we are getting better outcomes in cities where fewer dollars are being spent, then we are definitely paying too much in other cities.

Physicians have a deep knowledge base; they can define disease states accurately. And for some diseases time-tested treatments are available. For example, physicians know much about the human spine. They can show you MRI images of your spinal cord with all the defects that may be present from injury or chronic weakening of the tissues. If you have back pain and your MRI images show pressure on your spinal cord, the orthopedic surgeon can do surgery to relieve the pressure. But is back surgery always the best treatment? On this and scores of other medical conditions, medical experts differ in their opinions.

WHAT ARE PRACTICE GUIDELINES?

Medical researchers are now trying to determine what specific treatments produce the best outcomes for specific medical conditions. As the results become known, medical specialists are creating written outlines of the best treatment protocols to use.

In the health care industry, these written outlines are known as *practice guidelines, treatment protocols,* or *practice parameters.* They refer to a written description of what medical experts believe is the "best" clinical practice when treating a specific disease or medical condition.

Bill Petersen, M.D., medical director of the Health Outcomes Institute of Bloomington, Minnesota, says that practice guidelines are just that, guidelines. They are parameters designed to assist the physician in customizing patient care in the most appropriate manner.

HOW PRACTICE GUIDELINES BEGAN

In the 1970s a physician in New Hampshire began studying the variation in the ways physicians practiced medicine. In one of his celebrated reports, John Wennberg, M.D., of the Dartmouth Medical School showed the medical community that in some areas of the country tonsillectomies were performed much more often than in other areas of the country. He showed that the differences could not be explained by differences in the patients, but rather in the way physicians went about their work. In another study, he showed that prostate surgery was higher in some areas of the country than in others.

Then, in the 1980s the Rand Corporation reviewed thousands of Medicare medical records which showed that as much as 30 percent or more of certain medical procedures were inappropriately administered to patients. Some physicians, guarding the traditional territory of their various medical and surgical specialties, criticized the Rand Corporation reports. But others, interested in taking this type of research further, began studying the effectiveness of various treatment approaches to common medical conditions.

WHY PRACTICE GUIDELINES ARE USED

Not all clinical guidelines are expected to save managed care organizations money although most do because they reduce the amount of unnecessary care that is given when guidelines are not followed.

Practice guidelines are intended to be good medicine in the sense that the outcomes of treatment are expected to be better than if the guidelines were not used. At issue, though, is the definition of what is "better." Sometimes you and your physician may differ in your opinions of what is better. Better involves not only the fact that you are free of disease, but it also means that the quality of your life, as you define it, has improved. For example, if your physician recommends a certain treatment after surgery, you may or may not agree that the proposed treatment will result in a better quality of life. It all depends upon what you consider valuable—what you expect out of life after your treatment is over. See Figure 12-1 for advice on discussing practice guidelines with your physician.

Guidelines create more uniformity in how physicians practice medicine. Physicians are not *required* to use practice guidelines, and all guidelines have built-in flexibility to allow for individual differences in patients. It has been demonstrated that physicians who use guidelines do gradually change their behavior. In addi-

---

1. Ask your physician whether he or she uses a practice guideline for your medical condition.
2. If you find out that a practice guideline is used for your situation, ask to read a summary of it.
3. Discuss with your physician any differences your condition presents compared with what the practice guideline suggests.
4. If you disagree with what the guideline says about your condition and what to expect, discuss this with your physician.
5. Compare your health plan benefit agreement with the practice guideline that your physician is using. Make sure you understand what will and will not be paid for by your plan.
6. Read about your medical condition and compare what you find with what you are told regarding the practice guideline. The better informed you are about your own condition, the more involved you will be in your treatment and the better your chances will be of having a successful outcome.

FIGURE 12-1 Discussing a practice guideline with your physician.

tion, higher uniformity will help managed care organizations monitor cost effectiveness over larger populations.

In the future managed care organizations may use practice guidelines to conduct physician performance evaluations. This approach to managing care is so new, though, that it may be several years before guidelines are accepted enough to be used in evaluating your physician's work.

Managed care organizations look to practice guidelines to inform their utilization management work. For example, the criteria for determining the medical necessity for a diagnostic procedure such as ultrasound can be developed based on practice parameters for medical conditions where ultrasound is recommended as the best diagnostic tool.

An Example of a Practice Guideline

Unstable angina is a condition caused by atherosclerosis, or plaque building up in the walls of your coronary arteries. When blood flow decreases in these arteries you get chest pain, pain down your arm, and other symptoms. How severe is the condition? How risky is it? What are the chances that you have coronary artery disease? If you do have the disease, what treatment practices should your physician use to achieve the best outcomes? What medicines should be prescribed? Should you be given aspirin, nitroglycerin, beta blockers, or some other medicine? What dosage levels are the most appropriate? Should you be treated as an outpatient or should you be taken to the hospital intensive care unit? How soon should you return to the physician for evaluation? What precautions should you take? All these questions and more are addressed in a clinical practice guideline developed by the U.S. Department of Health and Human Services Agency for Health Care Policy and Research.

Using this or some other practice guideline developed for the condition of unstable angina, your physician will start by identifying the specific indicators of your condition. A series of interlinked questions are answered, called an *algorithm*, giving the physician confidence in a specific diagnosis.

Based on the initial information generated from diagnostic tests, the physician will then make a decision regarding the first course of treatment. You will receive certain types of medication depending on the test results. You will be monitored to see how you respond. If your chest pain does not go away after the first, more aggressive course of medical treatment, further tests will be performed to determine whether some other serious condition is causing the chest pain.

Your condition will continued to be monitored and further diagnostic tests will be completed, followed by a treatment program designed specifically for your case.

THE NEXT FEW YEARS

According to Bill Petersen, M.D., the technology currently exists to fully integrate the data gathering needed to research health outcomes and refine the practice guidelines currently under development. Within only a few years the information links will be in place to begin generating the kind of information we need to improve practice parameters. Delaying the process is the challenge of keeping confidential the contents of your medical records. During the next few years the concerns over medical ethics and legal requirements will square off with the goals of medical research and the drive toward efficiency.

Participating in Continuing Care Planning

In the past it was not uncommon for patients to stay a week or more in the hospital. When you stayed this long there was little need for special planning for the day you returned home from the hospital, since you probably had fully recovered by then.

This practice changed, though, when Medicare began paying hospitals a fixed amount for each medical condition. Reducing how long you stayed in the hospital created new challenges to the professional care team who needed to prepare you for going home. In fact, caregivers needed to begin planning for your discharge as soon as you arrived. This process is called *continuing care planning*, or *discharge planning*.

Continuing care planning involves:

1. Anticipating the level of care you will need after you leave the hospital
2. Informing and educating you and your family about your health situation and what to expect in the future
3. Coordinating with outside agencies or your family (which ever is appropriate) to have the care you need after you leave the hospital
4. Making arrangements for any special medical equipment or social services that you will need at home such as an oxygen system, walking aids, etc.
5. Following up with you by telephone to make sure that you understand your responsibilities
6. Monitoring the progress you make

WHY IS CONTINUING CARE PLANNING HELPFUL?

With continuing care planning you are a participant in the management of your care, not just a spectator. When the discharge planner brings you or your family information about your options, you are given a chance to respond to the options before you leave the hospital. Your suggestions are considered seriously.

Discharge planning reduces the risk of surprise when you leave the hospital. Knowing what you will experience, you will have increased confidence in your ability to recover quickly and you and your family will understand what "normal" recovery is like. When you experience uncomfortable symptoms related to your recovery, it is not as upsetting to you as it would be if you were not informed. And, importantly, you will also know when something urgent occurs requiring immediate medical attention.

Safe, reliable continuity of care is one of the most important reasons for discharge planning. For example, if you were sent home after major surgery without instructions and without anyone available to assist you in your care, you would be at risk of not being able to care for yourself adequately. Or, if you had a broken leg and no arrangements were made for a home visiting nurse to periodically check in on you, you might not get your bandages changed and an infection could set in.

Discharge planning also reduces the confusion among members of your care team. When done properly, discharge planning involves all members of your care team, including people from outside organizations who participate in your care after discharge. Duplication of effort can be eliminated as team members communicate. Fewer details fall through the cracks, and interruptions in your care are reduced or eliminated.

WHAT TO EXPECT FROM CONTINUING CARE PLANNING

Discharge planning is an important part of the hospital treatment process and it helps to have a thorough understanding of the process. Here is a list of services you can expect from your discharge planner:

1. A thorough evaluation of your needs. Discharge planners follow a process similar to that which nurses follow—assessment, planning, intervention, and evaluation of results. If you, a family member, your physician, or another care team member expresses a need on your behalf for certain services, the discharge planner will usually get involved to help find a solution.
2. Specific information about your medical condition or hospitalization and specific instructions about what to do when you return home. You should receive both a verbal and written list of tasks or self-care instructions to perform when you leave the hospital. The list should be easy to understand and you should have an opportunity to get clarification before you go home. For example, if you had major surgery, your care team should tell

you how to prevent infection in the wound, how to change bandages, how to recognize complications, and so forth.

4. A written discharge summary. The *discharge summary* is a document written and signed by your physician that contains information related to your hospitalization, including:
   a. Medications and supplies needed after discharge.
   b. Special dietary instructions that you should follow.
   c. Self-care activities, such as exercises and personal care routines.
   d. Explanations of other organizations that will assist in your care (home health agencies, hospice, skilled nursing facility, etc.).
   e. When and where you should visit your physician or other caregivers after you leave.
   f. A phone number where you can call to get more information.
   g. A medical/nursing assessment that describes your treatment options and the risks associated with each option. It should include your physician's expectations for the options recommended.

5. A discussion regarding your treatment options. In addition to the discharge summary, someone from your care team should also discuss the information with you in person. The options should be explained, your feedback should be obtained, and the consequences of not choosing any or all of the options should be described. Your caregivers are trained to promote informed consent. They have their own professional opinions as to what type of continuing care you should receive, but also respect and value your involvement in the decision. If your HMO has an experienced discharge planning department, you will probably know your post-discharge treatment options before you ever get to the hospital.

6. Finally, if you are not competent to decide or are incapacitated, your legal guardian will be informed and involved in the decisions for follow-up care. To be considered competent you must be at least 18 years of age (in most states), able to understand the information needed to make a decision, able to analyze the relevant alternatives, and able to communicate your decision to your care team.

Use Figure 13-1 as a checklist for your continuing care planning.

YOUR FAMILY MAY NEED TO BE INVOLVED

I have mentioned a few times that your family will probably be involved in the discharge planning process. Your family or legal guardian(s) can be a vital support to you after you leave the hospital. They can encourage you to follow

- Did you receive a copy of the written discharge summary?
- Do you understand what type of care you will need after you leave the hospital?
- Do you (and/or your family) understand your condition?
- If necessary, do your family members or legal guardians know how to care for you after you leave the hospital?
- What other organizations will be involved in your care after you leave the hospital?
     Home health company: _____
     Skilled nursing facility: _____
     Hospice care facility: _____
     Other: _____
- Will you need special medical equipment when you get home?
- Do you understand your medication treatment plan?
- Do you understand the level of activity you can expect after you leave the hospital?
- Will you be asked to perform exercises or other activities?
     If so, what are they? _____
     How often each day or each week?
- Will you be on a special diet? If so, are your dietary likes and dislikes considered for the special diet?
- Will you need to visit your physician after you get home?
     When is the first visit? Date _____ Time _____

FIGURE 13-1 Continuing care checklist.

through toward your goals. They can give you valuable feedback to help you monitor your progress. If you forget details of the care plan, family members can help you recall them. They can also act as liaison for your care team.

In many cases family members can even provide care. They can learn how to change bandages, assist you in exercising, and prepare your special dietary program. They can also coordinate plans with your professional caregivers by making logistical arrangements for you, such as transportation to the physician's office, arranging for delivery of medical equipment, or setting appointments for the visiting nurse.

WILL YOU BE DISCHARGED TOO SOON?

Perhaps you have heard a horror story of how an HMO member was discharged from the hospital too soon and suffered the consequences. With patients staying fewer days in the hospital under managed care, it is no wonder that people have concerns about this. How serious is this concern? What should you expect from the HMO treatment team? Should you worry about being discharged before you are ready to go home? This perspective should help you as you consider these questions.

All people in America have the right to be free of harm caused by the carelessness of others. Within the health care system, caregivers have both an explicit and implicit duty to not do harm to their patients. The duty of health care professionals requires them to adhere to the relevant standards of care as practiced in the community. A caregiver can breach this duty by either actively doing something harmful to the patient or by failing to act when action is appropriate.

It would be a violation of medical malpractice laws if a member of your care team did not adhere to the standard of care under the circumstances as practiced in the community. Your team is required to treat you, an HMO member, no differently than other patients are treated.

Your physician's duty prohibits him or her from abandoning you by discharging you before you are medically ready. When you no longer need acute care services, and after your care team has made reasonable steps to implement a continuing treatment plan, then you should be discharged as long as this will not likely result in negative consequences to you.

Deciding that you are ready for discharge is a collaborative process involving everyone on the care team even though it is the physician who signs the discharge order and who is legally responsible for your care. Other team members have an obligation to advise the physician of your condition and to warn the physician if, in their opinion, you are not ready for discharge.

If you are worried that you may be discharged too soon, talk about this concern with your physician and your nurses. Ask them for more information about your condition and the experiences of others who have had the same medical condition. If the physician wants to send you home and you feel you will need more medical care than can be given you there, negotiate the decision. For example, you might ask to be transferred to a sub-acute care facility for a day or two before you go home.

Being ill and recovering from an illness or surgery is no picnic. It is impossible to assure you that you will have an ideal situation when you leave the hospital. Your health plan and hospital cannot guarantee that you will enjoy being at a skilled nursing facility for a few days. There is no way to ensure that your home nursing care will be completely satisfactory. However, your physician in collaboration with your care team will make a recommendation based on their experience working with these types of organizations for hundreds of patients just like yourself.

Above all, as I have pointed out before, *participate in the process.* Stay involved and communicate your point of view. Don't assume that there is just one way to accomplish the same objective. If you do not like your care team's discharge recommendation, participate in the discussion until you reach agreement.

POTENTIAL PROBLEMS IN CONTINUING CARE PLANNING

When discharge planning works smoothly, the transition from the hospital to your home or to another organization is almost effortless. However, in even the most experienced discharge planning systems things can sometimes go wrong. You can minimize the chances of this happening by participating actively in the discharge planning process with your care team. You have an obligation to yourself to monitor how well this process is working before you leave the hospital.

Here are some warning signs that your discharge planning process needs improvement:

1. You get the information you need but are not sure what to do with it.
2. You know what you are supposed to do, but you have not learned the skills required to fulfill the tasks.
3. Written instructions are temporarily out of stock.
4. You realize that your expectations are not the same as your treatment team's expectations.
5. The nurse who gives you the discharge information is a temporary staff person and appears to not know the details.
6. Information you hear from one member of your care team contradicts what other team members have told you.
7. Your family members or legal guardians are not included in the discussions.
8. You are too sick or too tired to pay attention to the discharge planning instructions.
9. You find out that your care team has not had a team meeting to confirm the details of your follow-up care.
10. Your nurse is too overwhelmed with responsibilities to give you the information you need.
11. The day before you expect to be discharged you find out that no one has made the necessary arrangements.

How confident you are in your own ability to respond to your situation is a good predictor of how well you will achieve your treatment goals. If you believe that you are able to perform the exercises, change your diet, and take the medications, you are more likely to give your best effort to follow through on your continuing care plan.

BE AWARE OF LONG-TERM CARE

Your continuing care may require you to transfer to another facility for long-term care. Be aware that this can create serious financial implications. For example, if you have a disability that requires you to receive skilled nursing care, your health plan may pay for a specific number of days—you will be responsible for paying the rest out of your own savings. Then, if the cash runs out and you still need hospital or long-term care services, you may have to sign up to become a Medicaid beneficiary.

Be prepared. Get advice from your continuing care planner. Contact a lawyer about estate planning. These preparations can protect you financially from having to take drastic measures in the event that you need long-term care.

CHAPTER 14

Managing Your Own Care

Managed care is built on a few uncompromising principles. One of the most important principles is that, as a health plan member, you have an active role in the process of maintaining your own health. Managed care plans realize that they have tremendous leverage for health maintenance when health plan members are active participants in appropriate self care. They are developing formal and informal ways in which health plan members can participate in this maintenance. Some of these include encouraging members to engage in health promotion and disease prevention activities and to collaborate in and to follow the medical advice provided by the managed care team.

SELF CARE

You probably do more for yourself than the rest of your managed care team does. They may be medical and nursing experts, but you live and care for yourself every hour of every day.

Self care is the single most cost effective means of improving health and the quality of life. If you added up all the resources spent for health care, probably 75 percent of the care you receive is care that you give yourself, or care that your family provides you. This includes all the health promotion and disease prevention activities you engage in. It also includes the care you give yourself or your family members during minor illnesses and injuries. Even if you have a chronic condition, you do most of the monitoring of your own health status, including medication management, nutrition, exercise, and home treatments.

HEALTH PROMOTION AND DISEASE PREVENTION

John Renner, M.D., president of the Consumer Health Information Research Institute in Independence, Missouri, cautions that we can take self care too far, and that a few simple, practical steps can be taken to promote your own good health. A long-time advocate of informed self care, Dr. Renner says you don't need to learn about all of the chronic illnesses; everybody doesn't get all of them. You don't have to call a physician every day on the telephone, but it helps to have someone, a friend or relative, with whom you can discuss health concerns. Many homes still do not have a good medical reference book, yet this can be more important, says Dr. Renner, than having a restaurant guide or a music library.

Here are a few good books to have in your home self-care library:

1. A book on home remedies
2. A book on where to call toll-free for information on a variety of health topics
3. A reference book on the side effects of medications and drug-to-drug interactions
4. A book on preventing disease

Dr. Renner agrees with many health maintenance experts that the two most dangerous things that people do are smoking and consuming alcohol. He comments that, as a nation, we've learned how to be fairly honest with ourselves about smoking, recognizing it as a preventable health hazard. But most people are still pretty deceptive about their drinking, and are not as willing to face up to the negative effects of alcohol use.

In addition, there are many other ways you, as a health plan member, can promote health and prevent disease. Proper nutrition, regular exercise, stress management, and adequate amounts of rest and water all promote good health.

COLLABORATION AND COMPLIANCE

No matter what your pain or discomfort, you visit your physician to get an explanation of what is wrong, why it is wrong, and what can be done about it. For example, you may visit your physician because you have trouble breathing. Your physician conducts a medical history, completes a physical examination, and performs a pulmonary function test. At the conclusion of the tests she announces to you that you have "chronic obstructive pulmonary disease." She explains that this problem is caused by years of smoking cigarettes. Then she gives you the medical advice: stop smoking. This is what can be done to change your breathing problem.

Medical advice comes in two forms: *proscription* and *prescription*. One the one hand, *proscription* is medical advice that tells you to avoid engaging in certain behaviors which place you at increased risk of disease or injury. In the previous example, the physician proscribes cigarette smoking. Other proscriptions include "don't drink and drive," "stop drinking alcohol altogether," and "avoid a high-fat diet." On the other hand, *prescription* is medical advice which directs you to engage in specific behavior designed to improve your health, relieve unpleasant symptoms, or cure a disease. Examples of prescriptions include advice such as "adhere to a strict diet and daily insulin therapy," "wear a safety belt while driving or riding in a car," "perform these physical exercises for your sore neck three times each day for the next two weeks," and "take penicillin pills twice a day for ten days to destroy the bacterial infection."

When you receive medical advice you make a judgment about the value of that advice and then you decide what to do about it. Making such a decision may not be easy especially since you are probably not trained in a medical field. For some illnesses and injuries the recommended treatments are crystal clear. But for other conditions the recommended treatments are debated even among physicians. So how do you know what is the best course of action? How can you improve the quality of your care?

In some cases, not following your physician's orders can jeopardize your well-being and increase your risk of a more serious condition. It can increase the costs of care if repeat tests or more expensive treatments are required later because of your decision. Noncompliance can interfere with your physician's best efforts. It can increase your discomfort or even the uncertainty of the health outcomes.

Sometimes, by not following medical advice you can avoid unwanted side effects. But while doing so may save money and time in the short term, it may or may not be the most beneficial in the long run. There are many questions about medical treatment options that have not been answered. Only after honest discussion with your treatment team can you decide upon the best course of action to follow.

The important point here is that you remain actively involved with your physician in making medical decisions. Figure 14-1 lists the benefits of being actively involved in your medical decisions, and Figure 14-2 gives tips on how to work closely with your primary care physician.

When you are more actively involved in your medical decisions, you:

1. are more satisfied with the care you receive,
2. are more satisfied about the outcomes of treatment,
3. are better informed about what to expect,
4. have the freedom to change the course of treatment once it has begun,
5. encourage your treatment team to be vigorous,
6. reduce the risks of error, and
7. increase the dignity of the whole health care experience.

FIGURE 14-1   The benefits of being involved in your medical decisions.

1. Ask your primary care physician for reports on your progress during an illness.
2. Tell your primary care physician any personal, religious, or cultural values that affect how you want to be treated.
3. If you know that you have a minor ailment but want to get some advice on what to do about it, ask to first see the physician assistant or nurse practitioner.
4. Ask for a full explanation of your health status — your physician owes you this. If you do not understand some of the details, ask for clarification.
5. If you are not satisfied with the information you get, ask for a second opinion. Your primary care physician will be able to help you find a physician for the second opinion.
6. Ask to speak with the medical director of the medical group or HMO if, after you have made your best effort to establish dialogue with the primary care physician, you wish to change to a different primary care physician. Remember that it is best not to switch primary care physicians too often.
7. Regularly complete patient survey forms. This is the best way to communicate with the medical director regarding how you feel about your care.
8. If you think of alternative treatments that are cost-effective, give your suggestions to your physician.
9. Keep your medical appointments.

FIGURE 14-2   Tips on how to work closely with your primary care physician.

THE HIGH RISK OF NONCOMPLIANCE

Medical research shows that patients fail to follow short-term medication programs 20 to 30 percent of the time. Patients who are given advice to prevent a disease for which they are at risk fail to follow medical advice 30 to 40 percent of the time. And patients with chronic illnesses fail to follow medical advice up to 50 percent of the time when the diagnosis is first made, although they tend to improve their ability to follow advice over time.

Even when a physician's advice is crucial to improving the quality of their medical care, why do many people not adhere to their physician's orders? Here are the most common factors that influence whether you will follow your physician's advice:

1. Your memory of previous experiences. You may have strong feelings about previous medical experiences that either encourage or discourage you from following your physician's recommendations.
2. Your beliefs about illness. If you feel that you can influence the outcome of your illness you are more likely to follow your physician's recommendations. Or, if the advice is consistent with your religious beliefs, you will likely follow your physician's advice.

3. Your relationship with the physician. A collaborative relationship usually increases the tendency to follow the recommended actions.
4. Your knowledge of your medical condition. The more you know, the more you will be willing to comply with the physician's orders.
5. Your knowledge of how and why the treatment works. The more you know about how the prescribed therapy works, the more you will want to see it work for you.
6. How complicated the instructions are. If instructions are simple to follow, you are more likely to follow them.
7. How many instructions you receive at one time. If you receive too many instructions at one time, you may forget some of the important ones.
8. Whether you can financially afford the therapy.
9. Your social support system. If you have supportive family and friends, you will more likely follow your treatment team's advice.
10. How much you trust the physician. Higher trust means more collaboration and more use of the prescribed treatments.
11. Known or feared side effects of the recommended treatment.
12. The degree to which you will be required to change your lifestyle as a result of the advice.
13. Whether you feel embarrassed about performing the recommended activities.
14. How much of a burden you feel that you place on others by following the advice.
15. Your willingness to submit to the medical authority of the physician.
16. Your willingness to accept your illness and its consequences.
17. The psychological cost of enduring pain, disfigurement, or the hazards of treatment.
18. Whether the symptoms go away after you begin the treatment.

Use this list to identify your own feelings about your physician's orders. If you find that you are resisting advice you have been given, some of this may fade as you explore these feelings with your family, physician, or nurse. See Figure 14-3 for how to do your own research into your treatment options.

GETTING A SECOND OPINION

You may not agree with everything that your physician says about your condition and how to treat it. If you feel strongly about your own opinion on your condition, discuss this openly with your physician. If during such a discussion you still

If you question your physician's advice, research your physician's orders for yourself to satisfy your curiosity. You can:

1. Consult with your pharmacist for information about medications.
2. Ask a librarian to help you search for relevant articles describing your condition and the best treatments available.
3. If you are a subscriber to an on-line computer service, consult the health information section for information on medications.
4. Many treatment options are negotiable. Discuss your situation with your physician.
5. Discuss your religious beliefs with your physician.
6. Ask your physician for specific examples of self-care activities you can do for your condition.

FIGURE 14-3   How to do your own research into treatment options.

do not come to agreement with your physician, you owe it to yourself to get a second opinion.

A request for a second opinion should be welcomed by your physician. Most health plans who want their members to be active participants in the care process will agree on this point. Yet, many health plan members do not use the second opinion as often as they might.

To request a second opinion, first state your request to your primary care physician. If your request is not approved within a few days, repeat the request and contact the member services department. If after the second attempt you still have not received a response, ask to speak with the medical director. Be aware that the second opinion will be provided by a physician who is associated with your health plan.

Asking for a second opinion is just one of many ways to be involved in managing your own care. If you are not sure how to do this or have any other questions about how to participate in managing your care, talk with your physician or the health plan member services department.

CHAPTER 15

Managing Medical Emergencies

If you wait until you have an emergency to learn how your health plan works, you probably have waited too long. David Siegel, M.D., medical director of Health Alliance Plan in Detroit, Michigan, recommends that when you first join your HMO you should read through the health plan literature and think about how you would handle a situation where you need care quickly. Imagine, for example, that your child has just fallen down and cut his lip open. Do you call your primary care physician? Do you go to a health plan urgent care center? A little forethought will prevent indecision—and possible more serious consequences during the emergency.

When you make the first visit to your primary care physician, include how emergencies are handled in your list of topics to discuss. Sometimes your physician may have extra information regarding emergency situations. Another approach is to call the health plan member information line and ask them to explain how emergencies are handled. The member services department will be able to help you identify the closest hospital that the plan uses and whether there is an urgent care center close to you. It will also be able to confirm for you any financial obligations you have when using the emergency room.

Dr. Siegel and other health plan medical directors suggest that many aggravations and problems can be prevented if HMO members would just take a few minutes to become familiar with this one issue. All health plans lament the problem that new members often do not read their health plan materials before a problem arises.

WHY THE CONCERN OVER EMERGENCY ROOM USE?

Emergency rooms are designed to care for true emergencies. If you go to the emergency room for your runny nose and sore throat, you will have to wait until the emergency room nurses and physicians have taken care of those with emergencies. For minor ailments, it is much better to call your primary care physician's office or the health plan for advice. You will probably get help sooner, and, more importantly, will allow the emergency room physicians to focus on patients who truly need immediate attention.

You will also get better continuity of care in non-life threatening situations if you call your physician first. Your physician knows your medical history; for example, you may have a chronic condition that is a factor in your emergency treatment. The physician's office also has your medical records on file. The hospital emergency room physician, on the other hand, has very little knowledge about you.

WHEN TO CALL YOUR PRIMARY CARE PHYSICIAN

If you have a non-life threatening situation, call your physician before calling 911. Here are some examples of when to call your physician:

- Any time you have a question about your health status
- Injury to a bone or joint but you are not sure whether it is broken
- Sudden, unexplained swelling, redness, or pain
- Numbness or tingling in extremities
- Pain that persists for more than a week
- You are unable to move or get up after falling
- Self-care activities do no good
- A cough that persists for more than 7 to 10 days
- Difficulty urinating; uncontrolled urination (incontinence)
- Sputum that is green, yellow, or rusty brown
- Coughing or vomiting up blood
- Blood in the urine or stool
- Headache pain that does not go away with self care
- Dizziness or confusion
- Sudden, irregular heart beat rhythm
- Severe and unexpected pain from exercise
- Sudden swelling of muscles
- Sudden double vision or blurred vision
- Unexplained pain in the lower abdomen
- Persistent vomiting or diarrhea for more than 8 hours
- Your skin becomes yellowish in tint
- You get an unpleasant reaction after taking a medication
- Sudden unexplained weight loss or weight gain
- Dog bite
- Puncture wounds and deep lacerations

If you are unable to speak with your physician, call the health plan 24-hour tele-phone line. If the problem rapidly gets worse, call 911.

URGENT SITUATIONS

Unfortunately, many people are simply not able to clearly define what constitutes an urgent situation. Bartley Yee, D.O., considers an urgent situation as:

> you say "I've got a problem." It may have been going on for a short time or a long time, but it has gotten to the point where you don't want to wait for something to be done about it. You feel like you need something done very soon about it. That is a judgment that, in many cases, you make for yourself. In some cases it is, "I don't want to wait until the physician's office opens tomorrow because I've got a problem that I think I need to be seen for tonight." Because of the your unfamiliarity with the problem, you may not know any better. You just know that something is wrong and you want to go somewhere to be treated.

When this happens, a couple of options are available to you. This type of situation is ideally suited for an evening and weekend clinic or urgent care center where you can be evaluated by a nurse or physician to determine how serious your condition is. You could also call a health plan 24-hour telephone line for advice.

EMERGENCY SITUATIONS

As you know, other situations are much more serious. Dr. Yee recommends that health plan members think of an emergency as

> any situation that is life threatening, rapidly changing with no endpoint in sight. Here you have a situation that is suspicious for a potentially dangerous, possibly fatal prob-lem that without any intervention may rapidly move toward death. Unfortunately there are a lot of situations that cannot be clearly lumped into this one group. Each situation has to be defined for itself. And then someone with experience and knowledge has to make a clinical judgment about whether or not you need medical attention. In a case where you are having a significant problem, if you cannot find someone to help you with it, most health plans are saying, "go ahead and go to the emergency room."

The spectrum of people varies widely in how they define a serious situation. Some people think that a body temperature of 104 degrees is no problem. Others think that they should go to the emergency room when they get a sore throat.

This is where a good health plan patient education program can help you understand what can be done on your own.

Some situations are so serious that immediate medical attention is required. These include:

- Heart attack
- Severe chest pain
- Pulse rate is constantly high (above 140 beats per minute)
- Respiration rate is constantly high (above 28 breaths per minute)
- Lack of breathing, severe difficulty breathing, or blockage of your airways
- Drowning
- Fainting or loss of consciousness from any cause
- Poisoning or exposure to any toxic substance
- Uncontrolled bleeding
- Seizures or convulsions
- High fever (higher than 102 degrees Fahrenheit—38.9 degrees centigrade—for more than 30 minutes)
- Severe dehydration from vomiting or diarrhea
- Burns
- Head injuries
- Neck or back injuries where the spinal cord may be injured
- Bone fractures
- Eye injuries
- Heat stroke or heat exhaustion
- Hypothermia (low body temperature from exposure to cold)
- Severe frost bite
- Gun shot wounds
- Diabetes or insulin reaction
- Extreme weakness
- Loss of the use of any body part; loss of speech, hearing, sight, or motion in any extremity
- Severe, incapacitating pain
- Bleeding from the ears or mouth

If you or someone you are with experiences any one of these, call 911 immediately.

The Authorization Process for Emergencies

If you go to an emergency room, the emergency room admitting clerk will need to see your health plan identification card. If you do not have your card with you, tell the clerk the name of your health plan or the name of your managed care physician. If you are in a life threatening situation, the emergency room physicians and nurses will provide treatment immediately and ask questions later.

The clerk will then call either your physician or your health plan to verify that you are an eligible member. Someone from the emergency room staff will also give either your physician or your health plan the information about your case in order to obtain authorization for the care that is being provided to you. In this type of situation when it is medically necessary to provide you with care, authorization will be given.

If your situation is not life threatening, your medical group or health plan still will be contacted for authorization. You may be instructed to either stay at the hospital emergency department or go somewhere else for treatment. If you can be seen by your physician or at a designated urgent care center or clinic, the hospital emergency department may or may not obtain authorization to provide treatment for you.

You will be informed if the emergency department is not authorized to treat you. In this case you will choose whether to stay at the hospital for care or follow the request of your health plan or physician. If you stay at the hospital, be aware that you may have to pay for services out of your own pocket. This is one of the things you should ask your health plan when you enroll so you will know what to expect.

Monitoring Patterns of Emergency Room Use

Your health plan carefully monitors use of the hospital emergency rooms. If the plan or your physician notices that you are a frequent user of the emergency department, you may be given information on how your health plan works and how to use the system. If you persist in using the emergency room when you could be using your physician's office or a designated clinic, you may be assigned to a case manager who will monitor your care more closely.

Out-of-Area Emergencies

All this may work well when you are in the area where your physicians and hospitals are located. But what about when you go on a trip out of the area? What should you do if an emergency arises then?

First, let's define what "out of area" means. Sometimes called "out of network," this is the area outside the immediate area served by your health plan. Sometimes the area served is defined by drawing a circle on a map of the area surrounding your physician's office or the health plan's main hospital. Each health plan defines its own service area differently—the circle could have a thirty-mile radius, or it could be significantly smaller or larger.

If you have a life threatening emergency while out of the health plan's service area, call 911 or go to the nearest hospital emergency room or medical facility. Health plans want to be notified as soon as possible that you did receive care at a facility out of the area. If you have your health plan identification card with you, the hospital emergency room can contact your health plan more easily and quickly to inform it about your situation and to obtain authorization for treatment.

THE BIGGEST PROBLEM HEALTH PLANS FACE

All the recommendations listed here are based on the assumption that you or someone with you recognizes that you have a problem. Bartley Yee says that one of the biggest problems is

> people who, for whatever reason, do not recognize that they have a significant problem, or they deny it and it continues to get worse without any medical intervention. And then all of a sudden, the catastrophic problem occurs and they are in serious trouble needing to go to the hospital emergency room.

Be aware of what is normal and not normal for your body. Stay in contact with your physician. Learn all you can about your health plan's policies regarding emergency room use. See Figure 15-1 for a checklist of what you can do to help manage emergencies.

1. Read your health plan materials regarding emergencies.
2. Practice good safety measures to prevent accidents from falls, fire, and violence.
3. Get basic training in first aid and CPR.
4. If you or your family member has a sudden onset of an unexplained illness, don't wait until the situation becomes life threatening. Call your primary care physician's office for advice.
5. Be prepared. Keep the telephone number for your primary care physician or your clinic near or on the telephone.
6. Find out the hours your physician's office is open each day of the week. Write a summary of this on the card that you keep near the telephone.
7. Identify what location you can go to for after-hours care in the evenings and on the weekends. Write on your card the addresses and telephone numbers of these facilities.
8. Know the boundaries of your health plan's service area and use the facilities within the service area whenever possible.
9. Know your financial obligations when using the emergency room within the service area and outside the service area. What copayments are required for each type of situation?
10. If you travel, be sure to carry the following items:
    a. Your health plan identification card
    b. Your physician's name, address, and telephone number
11. If you are going on an extended trip that will last more than a week or two, contact your primary care physician's office before your departure to inform the office of the area in which you will be traveling.
12. If you routinely go away for the winter months you should do the following:
    a. Contact your health plan member services department for special instructions. Your health plan may have formal relationships with physicians and hospitals in the town you will be in. If not, your health plan will tell you what to do.
    b. Have a copy of your medical records sent to a physician in the area you will be in during the winter.

FIGURE 15-1   Checklist for managing emergencies.

CHAPTER 16

Planning for the Improbable: Advance Directives

Most of your life you are free from serious illness, so it is easy to forget how difficult and how complicated life can become if you have to go to the hospital. It would be nice to think that your physician and nurses will take care of you until you are well enough to go home, and then everything will be fine. But this is not necessarily always the case.

If you are like most people, you probably have a difficult time conceiving of a situation in which you are so sick that you cannot make your own health care decisions. I'm not superstitious, but I work in a hospital every day and even I hate to think about the improbable happening, much less plan ahead in case such an event does occur. I don't think I am alone. As ironic as it sounds, the reason you do not plan ahead is the very reason you *should* plan ahead.

MAKING YOUR WISHES KNOWN

You cannot be certain about your health care needs in the future, but you can do some planning in advance so that in the unlikely event that you are unable to make health care decisions or make them known, you can rest assured that your managed care team will follow your directions.

This planning process is called making an *advance directive*. This is a decision about the medical treatment you want made in advance of when you may need it. And it is a directive that you give to others so that they know what your wishes are.

Having an advance directive is one of your basic rights as a patient in the American health care system. You don't have to be an HMO member to prepare an advance directive. However, HMOs promote the use of advance directives because these documents keep you involved in your care. They respect your right to decide. Advance directives can help simplify a difficult situation for everyone by giving your physician the legal authority he or she needs to carry out your desires.

THE TWO OPTIONS FOR ADVANCE DIRECTIVES

In many states you have two forms with which you can express your advance directives, the living will and the durable power of attorney. The *living will* is a legal document that describes the medical treatments you want or don't want if you have a terminal illness or a medical condition from which you are not expected to recover. A *durable power of attorney* is a legal document in which you designate a person who will make your medical decisions for you if you cannot express your desires yourself. See Figure 16-1 for a sample durable power of attorney document. Some states recognize only one form, which may include both concepts. Check your state regulations to find out about your options.

WRITING YOUR LIVING WILL

A living will can be an official document that an attorney can write for you. It can be a form that a local hospital gives you, or it simply can be a written description, in your own words, of what you want done for you if you are unable to express your desires on your own. Using a prepared form can reduce the chances of misunderstanding what you say in your own words. I suggest that you first discuss the idea of a living will with your physician so that when you write the document you will do so in a way that is clear.

Choosing an Agent

In a durable power of attorney document, the person you give the authority to make medical decisions for you is known as your *agent* (also called "the attorney-in-fact"). The document requires your agent to follow your advance directions as you have stated them in the document.

Not to be confused with the type of agent who represents movie stars and sports figures, your agent will have the power to consent to your physician's decision to not give treatment, withdraw consent for any treatment or procedure, or request that the physician stop treatment necessary to keep you alive.

Your agent should be a family member or a close friend who is at least 18 years of age or older. You should choose someone whom you can trust, who knows you well, and who has the courage to represent your interests when others may protest. Do not ask your physician to be your attorney-in-fact since he or she is legally prohibited from doing so anyway. Also, you may not select someone who works in the health care field or is an owner or employee of a health care facility, a community care facility, or a residential care facility. Also, you would, of course, only want to select someone who shares your opinions about health care treatment. Check your state regulations for other limitations on who can be your agent.

Talking With Your Designated Agent

Be sure to ask the permission of and get a commitment from the person you want to be your agent. Making such a request is an important step for both you and your agent, so allow adequate time to discuss what durable power of attorney involves. This will give both of you a chance to explore your feelings. Here are some of the issues to discuss with the person you select:

1. How you feel about health care
2. How you feel about the various treatment options
3. How you feel about the possible outcomes
4. What treatment you prefer for various circumstances
5. What your goals are if you are not able to make medical decisions
6. How you feel about autopsies and donating your body for transplants or for scientific research
7. The time frame you want the durable power of attorney to be in effect
8. That you may give a copy of the written document to your physician
9. Whether or not the person you select agrees to act as your attorney-in-fact
10. Whether this person will likely be available when needed
11. Your power to revoke durable power of attorney for any reason, at any time, without prejudice to your agent as long as you are competent to make this decision and to express it
12. Whether you have selected alternates, who they are, and whether or not they have accepted your request

After you and your designated agent have discussed the issues that are important to you, you need to ask for a commitment. If the person needs a little time to think it over, allow him or her a reasonable amount of time to do so—you may want to set a specific date so you can complete your plans expeditiously. If, after doing so, you do not hear from this person for a long time, offer to discuss the

I. By this document, I create a durable power of attorney by appointing the person named below to make health care decisions for me as allowed by state law. This power of attorney shall not be affected by my inability to make decisions in the future. By this document, I hereby revoke any prior durable power of attorney for health care. I am a resident of the State of _____ and am at least 18 years old. I create this durable power of attorney of my own free will and acting with a sound mind.

II. I, _____ the PRINCIPAL of this document, hereby appoint:

NAME: _____
ADDRESS: _____
WORK TELEPHONE: _____ HOME TELEPHONE: _____

as my agent (attorney-in-fact) to make health care decisions for me. This power of attorney shall remain in effect for an indefinite period of time or until such time as I revoke it or as limited in duration as follows:

This power of attorney shall expire on the following date:
_____.

III. Medical treatment desires and limitations

If I become incapable of giving informed consent or of making medical decisions, my agent has full power and authority to make those decisions on my behalf subject to the following limitations and directions:

_____
_____
_____
_____
_____
_____
_____

IV. Alternate Agents (OPTIONAL)

If the person named above as my agent is not able to fulfill or is unwilling to fulfill my request to act as attorney-in-fact for health care decisions as authorized in this document, I appoint the following alternate person to do so:

FIGURE 16-1 Sample durable power of attorney document.
Adapted from the California Medical Association Durable Power of Attorney for health care decisions, 1992. Used by permission.

NAME: _____

ADDRESS: _____

WORK TELEPHONE: _____ HOME TELEPHONE: _____

V. PHOTOCOPIES

I hereby authorize that photocopies of this document may be relied upon by my agent and others as though they were originals.

VI. SIGNATURE

I sign my name to this Durable Power of Attorney for health care at the following city and state: _____, _____ on this date _____.

_____

Signature of Principal

VII. WITNESSES

I declare under penalty of perjury under the laws of the State of _____ that the person who signed this document is personally known to be the principal, that the principal signed this document in my presence, that the person appears to be of sound mind and under no duress, fraud, or undue influence. I also declare that I am not the agent appointed as attorney-in-fact for health care by this document, that I am not a health care provider, an employee of a health care provider, the operator of a community care facility or a residential care facility for the elderly, nor an employee of or an operator of a community care facility or residential care facility for the elderly.

SIGNATURE _____   SIGNATURE _____

PRINT NAME _____   PRINT NAME _____

DATE _____   DATE _____

ADDRESS _____   ADDRESS _____

_____   _____

I further declare that I am not related to the principal by blood, marriage, or adoption, and to the best of my knowledge, I am not entitled to any part of the estate of the principal upon the death of the principal under a will now existing or by operation of law.

SIGNATURE OF ONE OF THE WITNESSES: _____

FIGURE 16-1   *(Continued)*

issues again. Acknowledge that you sense some hesitation and that you do not want him or her to feel pressured—you can always select someone else.

After you have secured an acceptance to your request, complete the durable power of attorney form or letter. You should keep a copy in a safe place. You should also give a copy to your agent and to your physician. If you talk with your physician, you may want to give him or her a summary of the issues discussed with your agent.

Talk to Your Family about Your Agent

It is best to discuss your selection of an agent with your family. Tell your family members whom you have selected, the specific requests you have made, and where the document is located that describes your wishes.

Even if your agent is a family member, do not assume that other family members share your views. With a frank discussion ahead of time, you can minimize the risks of family conflict if your agent ever needs to act on your behalf. A troublesome situation can arise when your agent needs to fulfill this legal obligation but a family member attempts to thwart his or her efforts. In a challenging situation such as this, your agent must be a strong person who can stand up for his or her legal rights and for your rights as a patient.

Making It Legal

After you have written your document or filled in the pre-written form, be sure to sign it. Some states require the signature of two witnesses who can attest to the validity of your request.

You should not have to worry after signing the document for you are free to change your mind later. If you do change your mind, you should prepare another written document stating that you have revoked the previous document and describe your new wishes. Make every effort to discuss your change of mind with your agent, your family, and your physician.

COMMON QUESTIONS AND ANSWERS

The following are answers to common questions. Check your local state regulations regarding durable power of attorney and living will for any variations.

1. *If I designate in writing an agent to act as my attorney-in-fact, does this mean that I give up my right to make my own medical decisions if I am still capable of doing so?* No. As long as you have the ability to make your own

decisions and to make these decisions known, your appointed agent does not have the power to decide for you. You appoint an agent ahead of time, but his or her services are not allowed unless you cannot decide for yourself.

2. *What if the agent I select attempts to act contrary to my stated desires?* If your care team identifies that your agent is trying to act contrary to your written desires, they can take your agent to court to have his or her power of attorney taken away. A court can take away power of attorney if the agent approves of something that is illegal, or even if the agent tries to do something that, in the opinion of your care team, is clearly contrary to your stated interests.

3. *Can I limit how long my designated agent acts in this capacity?* Yes. The power you assign to this person lasts either indefinitely or for a limited period of time that you specify. If you want a time-limited period, be sure to state this in writing including the date that the power of attorney ceases.

4. *Can I change my agent?* Yes. You can notify your agent that you are revoking the power of attorney. Or you can notify your physician that you are revoking the power of attorney. You do not have to put this change in writing, although doing so is highly recommended since it will minimize confusion and conflicts. It is best to not change agents too often since doing so can cause confusion, too.

5. *What can my agent do if I die?* Your agent may have the right to authorize an autopsy, donate your body or parts of your body for transplantation or for research, and make arrangements for burial. These powers are subject to any conditions that you specify in writing. For example, if you do not want an autopsy to be performed, you should state this in writing and your agent will not have the power to override your wishes. In the case of autopsy, you should be aware that local laws may preempt your desires in case you die from an unexplained cause.

6. *Should I notify someone else as to who my agent is?* Yes. You should notify your physician and other family members. Give them copies of the written documents that you prepare. Beyond this, no other people need to know whom you have selected. If you notify your physician, a note can be put in your file for use at a later date. Notifying your physician can reduce confusion and improve the speed with which your wishes are carried out in the future.

7. *Does my agent have the power of attorney for all decisions, including financial investments?* No. The medical durable power of attorney you sign is limited to health care and medical decisions.

8. *Can I choose two people to be agents for me?* The best choice is to select just one person. If you pick two people they could have a dispute over what

type of care you wanted. I recommend choosing one agent and an alternate in case your first choice is unable to fulfill the responsibility.

9. *Does my agent have the right to read my medical record and to release it to others?* Unless you limit this right in writing, your agent will be allowed to read your medical record and to consent to the release of your medical record to others.

10. *Can I choose an alternate agent in case my primary choice is unable to fulfill the responsibility?* In some states this may be possible. Be sure to check your state law.

11. *Are advance directives required by my physician or my health plan?* No. While most hospitals, health plans, and physicians will recommend that you prepare them, you are not required to do so.

12. *Can I prepare an advance directive after I am admitted to the hospital?* Yes, as long as you are able to understand your treatment options and express your wishes you can prepare advance directives any time.

13. *Can I have someone write them for me?* Yes, as long as you are able to tell the person what to write and then you sign the document. Someone else is not allowed to write an advance directive that you do not authorize.

TREATMENTS AND SERVICES

Even if you are unable to make your medical decisions known to your physician, you may still desire one of a variety of services to sustain your life and provide comfort. Here are some of the most common options you have which you can express in your living will:

CPR (Cardiopulmonary resuscitation): A procedure that someone will perform on you if your heart stops beating, CPR can keep you alive but it may not sustain your life. You may want CPR given under certain circumstances and not in others, or where the probable benefits outweigh the possible outcomes. It pays to be as specific as possible, but you can leave the final judgment up to your physician and appointed agent.

Intensive care unit: This is the hospital unit that closely monitors your heart and lungs and is where you may be put on a respirator or ventilator to assist you with breathing. Receiving the services of an intensive care unit can keep you alive, but it may not sustain your life. You may want respirator care for certain conditions but not in others.

Tube feeding: If you cannot swallow food or take in fluids to sustain life, you may be given nutrition through a tube or an intravenous (IV) line.

Kidney dialysis: If your kidneys cannot perform their function, you may be periodically hooked up to a dialysis machine that cleans the impurities from your blood.

Hospice care: If you are in the last stages of a terminal illness such as cancer or AIDS, hospice care is available to provide nutrition, fluids, and comfort.

Pain medication: No matter what condition you have, a variety of pain medications can be given to keep you comfortable, including narcotics such as morphine. You may want certain types of pain medication and not others.

No treatment: You always have the option to instruct your physician that you do not want any treatments if you are unable to make your medical decisions known.

BE AWARE OF POSSIBLE OUTCOMES

It pays to be aware of the risks of various unfortunate conditions that you can experience during care. In any type of surgery, there is a risk of unexpected complications. And there are numerous chronic conditions and diseases for which there are no known cures today. These conditions include congestive heart failure, diabetes, emphysema, cancer, and AIDS. In these cases, your managed care team can keep you comfortable and keep you alive, often for a long time, until your condition eventually worsens.

A managed care team can keep someone in an irreversible coma or a persistent vegetative state alive by use of a ventilator. However, irreversible brain damage often results in permanent loss of consciousness.

It is possible to recover from a coma but have severe brain damage. In this case special care is needed, such as someone to provide food and care, sometimes necessary through a tube or an IV line.

You should discuss some of these possibilities with your physician before you decide what you want to write in your document.

YOUR ORDERS TO THE PHYSICIAN

Once you have considered the various options that you face if you are unable to make a medical decision, either permanently or temporarily, you should document the various treatments that you want and do not want, and under what conditions. For example, you may write that you do not want life-sustaining care to be provided under certain conditions, often stated as "do not resuscitate." In contrast, you may write that you do want efforts to sustain your life except in extraordinary circumstances, or that you want efforts to sustain your life even if you are in a persistent vegetative state.

Once you decide what orders to give your physician, both you and your entire managed care team will benefit by having these advance directives at their disposal. If you want more information about advance directives, see Figure 16-2.

---

1. Ask someone in your local hospital admitting department, discharge planning department, or utilization management department to mail a copy of an advance directive to you.
2. Ask your HMO member services department, discharge planning department, or utilization review department. Or ask your primary care physician for an advance directive form.
3. Your state or county medical society.
4. The regional office of the
   American Association of Retired Persons (AARP)
   Legal Counsel for the Elderly
   601 E. Street NW
   Washington DC 20049
   (202) 434-2120
5. "Advance Medical Directives"
   Krames Communications
   1100 Grundy Lane
   San Bruno, CA 94066-3030
   (800) 333-3032
6. Choice in Dying
   200 Varick St., 10th Floor
   New York, NY 10014
   (800) 989-9455
7. Your local social security office or the regional office of Medicare in your area.
   Ask for the following publication:
   "Medicare and Advance Directives"
   Publication No. HCFA 02175
   U.S. Department of Health and Human Services
   Health Care Financing Administration
8. Ask your attorney for information about advance directives.

FIGURE 16-2   Where to get more information about advance directives.

C H A P T E R   1 7

Preventing and Resolving Problems

Millions of Americans are satisfied members of managed care plans, yet no reputable health plan in America can boast a zero dissatisfaction rate. Now and then unintended problems arise.

As complex as delivering and receiving health care is, it's surprising that more problems don't exist. Scores of separate professions are constantly interacting with each other. Add to this the imprecision of medical science, the never-ending challenges that arise when working with people, and the constantly moving target of consumer expectations and you have a situation that is at high risk for consumer problems.

WHY MANY PEOPLE DON'T COMPLAIN

Some patients do not complain to health care givers when they experience broken promises and unfulfilled expectations. Some feel that health care is a private matter. Many of us have been trained to keep confidential the information about our personal health. We may feel embarrassed when faced with the prospect of complaining, or feel anxious about how a complaint will be received. Or we may not feel that we have the training to judge whether the care we receive measures up to commonly accepted standards.

To overcome these obstacles, I suggest you follow these four steps when dealing with health plan problems:

1. Know your rights. (See Figure 17-1 for a summary.)
2. Do all you can to minimize the need to complain.
3. Use a carefully planned approach to resolving problems.
4. Use the grievance or appeal process when all else fails.

Though not comprehensive, here is a list of your rights as a member of a managed care plan:

1. The right of reasonable access to quality care
2. The right of access to prevention services
3. The right to participate in the decision-making process of care
4. The right to decide the type and intensity of care that is provided at the end of your life
5. The right to inform the health plan of complaints without fear of discrimination
6. The right to be treated with courtesy, honesty, fairness, and respect
7. The right to have your concerns addressed promptly
8. The right to read and understand your own medical record
9. The right to accept or refuse medical treatment
10. The right to have your family involved in your assessment, treatment, and continuing care
11. The right to be informed of research and teaching activities involved in your care and the right to reject participation in such activities
12. The right of personal privacy and confidentiality
13. The right to all benefits that the health plan agreed to when you joined
14. The right to have your claims, grievances, or appeals evaluated objectively
15. The right to the same standard of care that other patients receive

FIGURE 17-1   Know your rights.

HOW TO MINIMIZE THE NEED TO COMPLAIN

To minimize the need to complain, keep the following suggestions in mind (see Figure 17-2 for additional suggestions on how to keep problems from arising):

1. Get to know the key members of your care team before problems arise. You should make a point to meet the office manager, the nurse, physician assistant, customer service representative, billing clerk, and others. Learn about what health plan departments are available to assist you. (Refer back to Figure 5-2 for a list of departments.)
2. When you are given instructions, verbally repeat them back to your care giver to make sure you understand all the details.
3. Get clarification immediately when you do not understand something. For example, your physician gives you specific instructions about what to do to take care of yourself when you get home. But in attempting to comply with the instructions, you discover that you do not understand everything.

Before Joining the Plan:
1. Know the locations of physicians and clinics that you are most likely to use on a frequent basis.
2. Find out the hours of operations of the providers you are most likely will use. Are these hours convenient for you?
3. Analyze the hidden costs, such as out-of-pocket expenses and the time you spend receiving care.
4. Find out how to get information and then test the information hot lines before you join.

Soon after Joining the Plan:
1. Be sure you are aware of how the policy on out-of-area care works.
2. Know how your health plan covers your children if they are away at college.
3. Know how to use the hospital emergency room.
4. Get to know the exact location of your physician's office or health plan clinic.
5. Read your membership identification card.
6. Make sure that all family members and the baby-sitter know what to do in case of an emergency.

FIGURE 17-2 More suggestions on how to prevent problems.

What to do? Don't wait. Call the physician's office immediately and explain your need for clarification.

4. Ask detailed questions, and if someone gives you an instruction that you are not clear about, ask for clarification. Include such questions as: "I'm not sure of the reason for this, can you explain more about it?" "When will this event take place?" "Who will be involved?" "What are their names?" "When will I be told the results?" "Who will tell me?" "What specific results are you looking for?" "How will we know if the results will be helpful?"

5. Make written notes of significant health concerns and medical situations that arise. This will help you get clarification before a problem comes up. It will also assist if problems arise later.

6. Check your assumptions about what will happen in the future.

7. If a problem arises, *do not wait to act* thinking that someone else will see the problem and correct it for you. If you get a bill you don't think you should have gotten, call the billing department immediately and attempt to resolve the matter before making a complaint. Most complaints can be avoided by simply having a discussion with the person who is most directly involved with the situation.

8. Know the formal grievance procedures. Your health plan and most medical groups that serve managed care patients have their own policies. Get a written copy of the grievance policy and read it carefully. If there is some-

thing in the policy that you do not understand, get clarification immediately *before* a problem arises.

9. Read your health plan benefits. The more familiar you are with what your health plan covers and what it does not, the more your expectations will be in line with what the health plan and your physicians can deliver.

PROBLEMS THAT CAN BE PREVENTED OR RESOLVED

Some problems arise because a new health plan member is simply not familiar with managed care. Others arise because a breakdown in communication occurs. Still other problems occur when someone in your health plan or medical group makes an unintended mistake. Does this sound like the kinds of problems that occur in other service industries? There are many similarities.

Of course, you should not expect to have all the problems on the following list as a member of your health plan. In fact, if you are like most health plan subscribers, you may never experience any significant problems. Here are some of the more common problems that can arise:

1. You are confused by or unfamiliar with the utilization management system, the authorization protocols, or the controls on the use of services.
2. You are not familiar with the benefit plan or have unrealistic expectations of what the health plan will provide for you.
3. You don't develop a relationship with your primary care physician within the first few months of joining.
4. You learn about emergency services only *after* an emergency occurs.
5. You are frustrated by the quality of service, such as lack of responsiveness, miscommunication, and disrespect.
6. You are unhappy with the physician to whom you were assigned when you joined the plan.
7. Your health plan benefit agreement is confusing.
8. You get sick when traveling out of the area and don't know whether your health plan benefits cover the situation.
9. You go to a physician not in the network and ask for services but discover they are not paid for by the health plan.
10. Your health plan hours of service are not convenient for you.
11. You feel you are not listened to by your physician or your clinic manager.
12. You have to wait too long (on the phone, in the reception area) before receiving care.

13. Confusion occurs regarding copayments and other financial obligations.
14. You don't understand the grievance procedures, or the grievance procedures have not been disclosed to you.
15. You enroll in the plan but need to see the physician before you are issued an identification card.
16. You are a new member of an HMO for seniors but present your Medicare card to your physician instead of your health plan identification card.
17. You switch to an HMO but continue to see a specialist before you make contact with the primary care physician to which you were assigned.
18. You are unable to get an appointment to see a specialist in a timely manner.
19. You do not agree with your physician's recommendation.
20. You or your family member believe that poor quality of care was provided.

HOW TO COMPLAIN WITHOUT EMBARRASSMENT

If you experience a problem in spite of your efforts to either prevent it or resolve it quickly, it is best to follow a carefully planned approach when making a complaint. This will help you to solve the problem faster and with less frustration. You should attempt to solve problems with the individuals directly involved with your care. If your first attempt does not succeed in resolving the situation, follow these steps:

1. Identify the specific problem. If you have vague, confusing feelings, try to clarify your own feelings. Some service problems are complicated. Think about the specific nature of the problem that is upsetting to you. It may help you to write down specific details. Keep copies of correspondence, documents, and reports. Record specific names, dates, times, places, promises, and the factual details of relevant events.
2. Talk again with those directly involved before taking the problem up the chain of command. If this does not bring satisfaction, inform those directly involved that you intend to discuss the matter with the person at the next level of authority.
3. Before taking it further, ask yourself these questions: How important is this? How certain are the facts? Do I have *all* the facts? What is at stake? What am I really trying to do by making a complaint? Am I trying to solve a problem or simply trying to teach someone a lesson? How do I want the problem resolved? What is reasonable to expect?

4. Keep organized. Keep relevant documents in a central location for easy access. Resolution will generally come more quickly if you have the information available when you talk on the telephone or discuss the matter in person.
5. Avoid "terrorist activities." Don't use unsubstantiated allegations, derogatory remarks, or abusive language just to get the customer service manager's attention. This approach always slows down the resolution process and switches the focus from solving the central problem to dealing with your behavior.
6. Explain the situation clearly, without apology. Be courteous but firm.
7. Listen carefully to the information you receive. Many complaints can be resolved simply by hearing all the facts.
8. Be persistent. You may need to say, "If you are unable to help me with this situation, I have the time to take it further. Please direct me to the administration."
9. Agree upon specific time frames for responses to your questions and concerns. For example, ask: "When will you call the medical director?" "When can I expect your report on what she says regarding my concerns?" Get a specific commitment. Keep a record of what the commitment is and who makes the commitment to you.

Use Figure 17-3 to keep a record of whom to contact for customer service.

APPEALS AND GRIEVANCE PROCEDURES

In some organizations administrative problems and human relations problems are the areas where the most complaints are brought by health plan members. Ellen Eisner, director of member services for Harvard Community Health Plan in the Boston area, explains:

A complaint in our organization is something like "I waited too long at the pharmacy" or "The physician was rude to me." It has to do with staff attitudes and administrative service problems. The appeals process is specifically focused on hearing cases relating to the denial of claims for payment, requests for exceptions to the benefit agreement. For example, you went to the emergency room and did not get prior authorization. Your claim is denied and you have to pay for it yourself. Now you want to appeal this decision.

An important point here is that not every problem that occurs will result in the grievance process. Complaints are recorded and followed up. Grievances and appeals take a different, more formal track to resolution.

Filling in the blanks below will save you time and aggravation later.

Your Health Plan:

1. Customer service department phone number
   during business hours: _____
   after hours (evenings and weekends): _____

2. Name of customer service manager: _____

3. Name of local health plan administrator or operations director:
   _____

4. Hours of operation for customer service department:

Sunday	_____ a.m. to	_____ p.m.
Monday	_____ a.m. to	_____ p.m.
Tuesday	_____ a.m. to	_____ p.m.
Wednesday	_____ a.m. to	_____ p.m.
Thursday	_____ a.m. to	_____ p.m.
Friday	_____ a.m. to	_____ p.m.
Saturday	_____ a.m. to	_____ p.m.

Your Medical Group, Clinic, or Physician's Office:

1. Customer service department phone number
   during business hours: _____
   after hours (evenings and weekends): _____

2. Name of customer service representative: _____

3. Name of customer service manager: _____

4. Name of medical group administrator: _____

5. Hours of operation for customer service department:

Sunday	_____ a.m. to	_____ p.m.
Monday	_____ a.m. to	_____ p.m.
Tuesday	_____ a.m. to	_____ p.m.
Wednesday	_____ a.m. to	_____ p.m.
Thursday	_____ a.m. to	_____ p.m.
Friday	_____ a.m. to	_____ p.m.
Saturday	_____ a.m. to	_____ p.m.

6. Name of your physician: _____

FIGURE 17-3 Customer service worksheet.

Federal and state regulations require that every HMO must follow a formal written procedure by which members can appeal a health plan action without fear of discrimination. As a member, you should be informed when you enroll and once each year thereafter regarding the grievance procedure your health plan uses. This information should include a step-by-step guide on what to do and what to expect in response to complaints.

By the time a situation becomes a grievance 98 percent of everyone involved understands what the disagreement is. It may be a disagreement over the benefit that was purchased by the employer. In this case there is not a whole lot the health plan can do about the matter. Or it may be a difference of opinion about a regulation that the health plan has. Whatever your grievance, be sure to follow the step-by-step approach outlined in your health plan materials.

The first step in formal grievance is to complete a written record of the grievance. Most health plans use a form for this purpose. Forms should be available at every physician's or medical group office, hospital, and clinic as well as at the health plan's office. In addition, the health plan should have someone available who can assist you in completing the form. You may submit a grievance in person or in the mail. Since it is a formal process, I recommend that you mail the grievance by registered mail return receipt requested. In this way you have legal documentation that your grievance has been received.

When your health plan receives the form from you, it has an obligation to formally acknowledge this in writing. The grievance procedure will specify how many days the health plan has to respond to your complaint—a reasonable time is two to three days. However, if the complaint cannot be resolved within this time period, your health plan has an obligation to refer your complaint either to the medical director or the chief operating officer of the organization.

Some plans allow up to ten days for the medical director or top executive to attempt to obtain resolution. During this time you may be interviewed by one or both of these individuals. You may be asked to submit specific information to validate your complaint. If at this point the situation cannot be resolved to your satisfaction, the grievance will be automatically referred to a formal grievance committee for review along with a written record of what has transpired during the process.

Your complaint should be resolved within thirty days of being taken to the grievance committee and you should receive a written response within this period. If you are not satisfied with the response of the grievance committee, you always have the right to file a grievance with the state or federal organization that oversees managed care organizations. If you file a complaint with a government agency, be prepared to describe the steps you have followed in making a good-faith effort to resolve the matter with the health plan before involving the government agency. In some cases, if you have not filed a formal grievance with the health plan first, the government agency may direct you to that process before it gets involved.

HMOs are required to keep formal written records of grievances and their dispositions. Audits by external regulatory agencies always include a survey of the grievances and their dispositions.

DISENROLLING FROM AN HMO

Disenrollment from the health plan is usually the last resort. If you decide to disenroll, contact one or more of the following:

1. Your employer (if your health plan is offered through your employment)
2. The HMO member services department
3. Your HMO primary care physician
4. The appropriate social service agency for Medicare or Medicaid programs

Disenrollment procedures usually involve paperwork and conversations with health plan representatives. It may also involve seeking health insurance from another organization. Before you make the leap, try to determine whether and to what degree you are covered under another health plan (such as your spouse's or a fee-for-service plan) after you disenroll. Getting into a health plan is easy, but in some health plans the exit barriers are pretty high. If you feel like you are being required to climb Mt. Everest to get out of the plan, call the member services department and ask someone to walk you through the disenrollment process step by step.

If you are a Medicare or Medicaid HMO member, you may have to wait 30 to 45 days before the disenrollment request becomes effective. This is because the information must be given to the government agency and the computer records updated before you are contacted.

Most managed care plans today are not in the business of making a fast buck. Rather, they want your continued business over time. It is much more cost-efficient to keep you as a loyal, satisfied member than to spend the marketing dollars needed to replace you with a new member. They have a public image to enhance. For these and other reasons, you have leverage on your side. Respect this marketplace leverage, but don't fail to use it when you need to do so.

HMO Management, Now and in the Future

CHAPTER 18

Measuring and Managing Costs

YOUR CONTRIBUTION TO THE COST OF CARE

Imagine that you receive the news that starting today you get a fixed amount of money to use for food, clothing, rent, and utilities. This isn't really news, is it? At the end of the month there is barely enough money to buy a postage stamp. You try to put a little away for the rainy day, but it seems never to be enough. Oh, I forgot to tell you—you may not use credit cards, you may not get a loan, and you must pay your bills on time or the money is taken away.

You may not think that health plans have this same challenge month after month, but this is exactly what happens in managed care organizations. They live on a fixed income based upon a certain amount of money per member per month. They must put a little away for the rainy day. And they have to pay their bills on time; otherwise physicians and hospitals drop out of the provider networks, employers cancel their contracts, and the health plan goes out of business.

Premiums

One of the identifying characteristics of managed care organizations is that as a subscriber you pay a fixed amount of money each month whether the services you use are many or few. If your employer offers you a managed care plan he or she pays this fixed amount. If you are in a Medicare or Medicaid HMO, the government pays the amount. This fixed amount is called the *premium.*

For example, in some regions the monthly premium ·for an HMO offered through an employer group might be as low as $100 for an individual each month. With this $100 the health plan is responsible for paying all the health care services covered under the benefit agreement whether you are healthy or ill.

Medicare calculates how much it pays a managed care organization using a formula established by the U.S. Health Care Financing Administration. The formula takes into account the geographic region where you live, your age, your gender, and the average amount Medicare spends on a person of similar age and gender in a previous period of time. Then the government gives itself a 5 percent discount and gives the rest to the health plan each month you are enrolled.

Medicare HMO payments vary widely from state to state and county to county. In southern California, for example, Medicare payments to health plans may be as much as $500, but in other states the payment may be as low as $150 per month for each member enrolled in the plan. It is no surprise that in regions with the lowest Medicare payments there are fewer, if any, managed care plans willing to offer a Medicare option.

If you are in a Medicare managed care plan, you may be asked to pay a monthly premium to the health plan in addition to the premium the government pays. How much you pay varies widely from region to region. In some of the more competitive markets Medicare managed care plans do not charge a premium to members. In other regions you may pay as much as $100 each month.

Premiums are usually set based on the age and gender of the person (or group) for whom the premium is paid. Premiums for infants and seniors are usually higher than the average. Why? Both groups tend to use health care services more than the average. In fact, older Americans can use twice or three times the amount of services as do young adults. In addition, premiums in point-of-service plans are usually higher because you have the freedom to use physicians and hospitals outside the health plan network.

Deductibles

January of each year brings with it many traditions—New Year's celebrations and resolutions, a chance to make a new start. January also means that you start over with your annual health plan deductible.

A *deductible* is the amount of money you pay out of your own pocket before your health plan begins paying claims. This means that if you never receive health services during the year, you don't have to pay any deductible. If you stay well all year but get ill in December, you still must pay the deductible for the current year. Then if you need medical services again in January the following year, you must pay the deductible for that year.

Here's how a deductible works: If your deductible for physician care is $400 each year but your first claim for payment is worth only $250, then you pay the physician the full $250 out of your pocket and the health plan pays nothing. If your second claim for physician services during the year is also $250, then you pay $150 (the remainder of your deductible) and the health plan pays $100. From then on during that year the health plan pays claims according to its agreed upon policies.

Deductibles are figured into the formula that is used when calculating the premium you or your employer owes to the health plan. In general, the higher the deductible the lower the monthly premium and vice versa.

Some health plans have just one deductible covering both physician and hospital care. Other plans have two deductibles, one for physician care and one for hospital care. Not every managed care plan requires its members to pay an annual deductible. Deductibles in point-of-service plans are generally higher. So if you pick one of these options, make sure you know what the deductible requirements are when you enroll. Use Figure 18-1 when learning about your health plan's deductible requirements.

Copayments

Whether or not you are required to pay an annual deductible, your health plan may ask you to pay a certain amount each time you receive services. This is called a *copayment*. Copayments are made to the physician, hospital, pharmacy, or other organization that provides care for you. Figure 18-1 includes a checklist of copayments that your health plan may require.

Deductibles
- What is your annual deductible for physician services? _____ For hospital services? _____
- What is the total annual deductible you must pay? _____
- If you and members of your family are enrolled, what is the total deductible for the whole family? _____
- How much more is the deductible for the point-of-service option? _____
- Do you have a choice of what deductible to pay? _____

Copayments
- What are the required copayments for each of the following:
  _____ Primary care physician visits
  _____ Specialist visits
  _____ Prescription medicines
  _____ Admission to the hospital
  _____ Each day spent in the hospital
  _____ Admission to a skilled nursing facility
  _____ Each day spent in a skilled nursing facility
  _____ Ambulance service
  _____ Home nursing care
  _____ Other: _____
- How much more are the copayments when you use the point-of-service plan? _____

FIGURE 18-1   Checklist for deductibles and copayments.

While deductibles are paid each year, copayments are paid each time you use a health service allowed in your benefit agreement. Copayments are usually small fees ($5 to $25) for routine physician visits, but are higher ($25 to $150 or more) when using other services such as hospital emergency room services. For some high-cost services the copayment may be a percentage of the total cost of care. For example, in some plans you may pay as much as 20 percent of hospital expenses up to a yearly maximum of $1,000 or $2,000. Just as with premiums and deductibles, copayments in point-of-service plans are almost always higher.

WHAT IT COSTS TO RUN A HEALTH PLAN

Labor is the biggest element of health care costs. As in any service industry, health care is labor-intensive. The more people involved in caring for you at any given day or hour, the higher the cost.

When you visit your physician for a routine physical exam the following people will probably directly or indirectly be involved in the care you receive during your visit: the physician who examines you, the office nurse, a scheduler clerk, a medical records clerk, and the clinic administrator.

But if you are hospitalized you receive the services of many people whose work is integral to your case. This can include any of the following: physician, three or four nurses, medical laboratory technicians and phlebotomist, billing clerk, admitting clerk, medical records specialist, financial planner, infection control, nursing supervisor, pharmacist and pharmacist technician, social worker/ discharge planner, dietary aid, registered dietitian, biomedical engineering technician, housekeeping staff, other allied health professionals such as respiratory therapists, X-ray technicians, physical therapists, and a whole cluster of people who provide nonclinical services such as billing, medical records, utilization review, quality improvement, and hospital administration.

In addition to the clinical service costs, there are many other health plan overhead costs such as running a member services department, enrolling new members, managing the computer system, monitoring health plan finances, and managing the overall administrative operations of the organization.

HOW YOUR PREMIUM DOLLARS ARE SPENT

Most of the revenue health plans receive pays for medical care. A small percentage is needed for health plan administration. See Figure 18-2 for a breakdown of

Here is a general breakdown of how health plans spend their
premiums of $100 per member per month:

Hospital inpatient care	$25
Hospital outpatient care	10
Physician services	37
Prescription medications	8
Miscellaneous health services	7
Health plan administration	13
TOTAL	$100

The actual amount your plan spends will be different.

FIGURE 18-2 How your premium dollars are spent.

where the premium dollar goes. Many experts say that a health plan should spend
no more than 20 percent of its premium on administration. Cost-efficient plans
actually spend a lot less. In some cases administrative costs are as low as 10 percent, and in some cases slightly less.

If the health plan takes in $100 per member per month (sometimes called
simply "PMPM"), it may pay $25 to $35 for hospital care, $8 for medications, $35
to $40 to physicians, and $5 to $10 for other health services such as home health
care and medical equipment. The rest it keeps for administrative costs.

HOW HEALTH PLANS MANAGE COSTS

Managed care organizations constantly review the revenue and expenses associated with conducting business. Here are some of the most common items that
are monitored:

1. Adverse selection versus favorable selection of members. When a managed
   care plan enrolls a higher than average number of subscribers who are at
   high risk or unhealthy, the organization's costs usually are higher, known as
   adverse selection. Conversely, when a higher than average number of low-
   risk or healthy subscribers are brought into an organization, the result is
   usually lower costs, referred to as *favorable selection.*
2. New or increased benefits. The benefit agreement is the element in managed care that has the greatest influence on costs. When the benefit agreement adds benefits not previously offered, the health plan financial

managers closely monitor the effects of these changes on costs. And, when a certain benefit is dropped from the benefit agreement, the financial managers monitor these changes as well.

3. Changes in copayments and deductibles. In general, when a health plan requires subscribers to pay more out of pocket to receive covered services, the resulting costs to the health plan usually drop. It is a simple principle: When consumers have to pay more for each unit of service received, they tend to be more involved with and consider more seriously the decision of whether to seek care or not.

4. Changes in the competitive market. When subscribers are notified by their employer that their health plan will be changed soon, some people may use health care services either more or less just before the change. If the new plan is perceived to be less attractive, employees will tend to use the old plan more just before the change.

5. Actions of the physicians and hospitals. While most health care providers refer patients for diagnosis and treatment services within reasonable and normal limits, there are usually a few who, for even justified reasons, refer their patients to more services than the average. Overutilization and inappropriate utilization drive up costs.

6. Unusual and high-cost patient encounters. Whenever an unusual health care situation occurs, the costs of that situation are monitored carefully. This is true for members who are involved in accidents that leave them partially or fully disabled. Other examples of high-cost services include neonatal intensive care for low birth weight babies, organ transplants, open heart surgery, and bone marrow transplants.

7. Capitation, or shifting financial risk. Under a system called *capitation* (based on the concept of per capita or per person), the health plan pays the hospital an agreed upon amount per member per month. It also pays the physician group a different amount per member per month. Both the hospital and the physician group then have the financial responsibility to provide and pay for all the care you are allowed under your benefit agreement.

8. Selective contracting. The current trend is to select providers who, because of their experience, their reputation for high quality, and their pricing, will help a managed care plan save money. When a health plan can contract with a facility at a price that is considerably less than what other facilities charge, huge savings can be generated over time.

9. Educating members on how they can help keep costs down. See Figure 18-3 for a list of things that you can do to help your health plan keep costs down. Managed care organizations do not want you to avoid care that you need, but they want to work with you to make sure that you receive the most appropriate care in the most efficient way possible.

As a member of a managed care organization, you can help to play a key role in managing costs. Here are some of the ways:

1. Read your benefit agreement.
2. Show up for your appointments.
3. Explore with your physician the possibilities of using generic prescription medicines instead of name brand medicines.
4. Participate in medical decision making. You are the co-captain of your managed care team.
5. Learn how you can do more self care at home.
6. Adjust your lifestyle to avoid personal activities that adversely affect your well-being.
7. If you get ill, call your health plan immediately. Collaborate with your physician or primary care nurse on the best course of action to take.
8. If you have an urgent medical need, avoid waiting until late at night or on the weekend to contact your health plan.
9. Participate in health screening services that your health plan recommends. Early detection can save your life.
10. If you have a chronic condition, ask to be placed in a case management program.

FIGURE 18-3   How you can help keep costs down.

Measuring and Managing Quality

It's report card day in managed care. Managed care organizations have been around for decades and now they are being asked to give an overall account for the care that they provide.

As a consumer of health care you have the same interests in the process and outcomes of care as the team members who provide the care. For example, when you are in the emergency room you want to know what is going on. You want a calm, reasoned approach taken for your care both in a life-threatening situation like this and in your routine care. You want to know what will happen next and how quickly it will occur.

You may not be a trained physician, but you are able to judge quality when you experience it. You know whether or not you have gotten well after seeing your physician, and whether the symptoms go away after you receive treatment, whether you understand what you are told regarding your condition. You know whether your functioning has improved, whether your quality of life has improved, and whether you were treated with respect. Although quality of care is more than this (see Figure 19-1), you know when you have received it.

The information you have about your condition is different from the information the physician has. Your physician knows the technical details, such as your blood potassium and hematocrit levels, your systolic blood pressure, your blood pH, and your white blood counts. He or she knows when a surgical wound is healing, when you are unconscious, or when you have impaired breathing.

The point is that measuring quality is a collaborative effort: you need the information the physician and your managed care team has and they need the information you have. What you lack—the technical knowledge—your care team can provide, and what information your care team lacks in measuring quality— your personal judgment and feelings—you can provide.

Here is a short list of how health care industry experts define quality. Quality health care:

1. Achieves the best possible health outcomes for you
2. Helps you function to the best of your ability given your condition
3. Gives the most appropriate level of intensity for your needs at the time
4. Is culturally and linguistically appropriate for you
5. Involves your entire family if necessary
6. Is accessible and efficient
7. Is provided in the most appropriate setting
8. Is the least restrictive on your preferences
9. Meets the changing professional standards of care
10. Allows you to actively participate in clinical decisions
11. Is a continuous, coordinated, and collaborative effort by a skilled multi-disciplinary team
12. Is provided in a manner that respects you as a person
13. Promotes health and practices disease prevention

FIGURE 19-1   How health care experts define quality.

THE THREE ELEMENTS OF QUALITY

We know now what goes into judging the quality of care of an individual, but judging the quality of care that thousands of health plan members experience is much more complex. Fortunately, there are ways to estimate quality: First, quality is built into the very *structure* of an organization by how it is monitored, the documentation it gathers and reports to outside organizations. Second, quality is also measured by what a health care organization does for its members, in the *process* it follows in attempting to create value. Health plans that have the processes in place do their best to keep members well; however, process in itself does not guarantee quality. And third, quality is also the result of what your health plan achieves, the *outcomes*. Figure 19-2 depicts a summary of these three elements of quality.

STRUCTURAL MEASUREMENTS OF QUALITY

When an organization is accredited, it has structural features in place that make it more likely that quality of care will be encouraged and implemented. Structural

> 1. **Structural quality:** What the organization is
>
> 2. **Process quality:** What the organization does
>
> 3. **Outcomes quality:** What results are achieved

FIGURE 19-2   The three elements of quality health care.

quality is not a direct measure of health care quality but it is one of the usual starting points. Does accreditation mean anything significant to HMO members? Absolutely! Here's how.

Accreditation is the process by which independent reviewers, trained specifically for the task, act as your agents in evaluating an organization's quality. Accreditation reviewers check every vital area of a health care organization's performance. Their job is to uncover and report to the organization areas that meet certain industry quality standards and areas that need improvement.

Hospital Accreditation

Hospital accreditation is nothing new. What is new about hospital accreditation is the marked increased emphasis on quality improvement structures that the accrediting agency, the Joint Commission on the Accreditation of Health Care Organizations (JCAHO), requires. Here are a few examples where quality must be built into an organization that wants to achieve accreditation:

1. Clinical laboratory. Laboratory equipment must be calibrated or tested. Chemicals used during tests must be tested for freshness. Technicians are evaluated periodically for their skills.
2. Infection control. Documentation in writing must show the protocols that are used for educating hospital personnel regarding infection control, gathering samples for analysis, analyzing the samples, and communicating with all relevant managers on the status of infection rates.

3. Medical records. Specific information must be maintained in all patient records.

4. Pharmacy. Pharmacy accreditation inspections include an evaluation of the storage conditions for medicines, the quality and age of the medicines, and the supply of emergency medicines, as well as the documentation of the distribution, security, and administration of specially controlled medicines such as pain killers.

5. Improving organizational performance. Procedures must be documented showing how the organization as a whole tries to improve its performance.

6. Utilization review. Documentation must show how the organization identifies underutilization, overutilization, and inefficient utilization.

Health Plan Accreditation

Most managed care plans require that the participating hospitals be accredited. In turn, many employer groups are asking that the health plan and physician groups become accredited, too. The independent agency known as the National Committee on Quality Assurance (also referred to as the NCQA) was formed for the purpose of establishing and monitoring health plan and physician group performance. Now the NCQA is the most popular accrediting agency for health plans.

Margaret O'Kane, the executive director of the NCQA, explains that the agency is a partnership between health plans and the important stakeholders such as employer groups, consumers, and quality experts. The NCQA considers that health plans are responsible for managing the health of the whole population for which they provide care. Health plans should look at the common causes of disease that might be prevented or what kinds of chronic conditions exist in the population that the health plan serves. She comments that

> as a consumer, you want to know that the health plan has been selective about which physicians are in the plan. You want to know that the health plan monitors the physician's performance and that if a physician is not providing care that would be a good quality, that the plan takes steps to change that either by taking the physician out of the plan, in an extreme case, or by working with the physician to improve his or her performance.

This same assurance is not available in traditional health insurance plans.

Prevention, which will become more important in the future of health care, is becoming more important to the accrediting process. The NCQA expects the health plan to define what services plan members should receive by different age groups, and what methods the health plan uses to educate physicians and members to make sure that members are receiving the prevention services.

Member rights and member satisfaction are two other areas on which the reviewers focus. Accreditation reviewers analyze the health plan's complaint gathering system as well as the actual complaints (and how these were resolved) that have been filed by members. How complaints are handled is a good window into what is working and not working for the health plan.

Reviewers for the NCQA actually go into the physician's offices and audit the medical records. They look at the quality and completeness of the records. They also look at the quality and appropriateness of care that is provided as documented in the patient records.

Sixty indicators of quality are used by the NCQA to monitor a health plan's performance. These are constantly under refinement to reflect the latest medical research. Examples include the number of children who receive immunizations, the number of women who receive Pap smears, the number of members who receive cholesterol tests, and whether the health plan has formal methods to identify its own areas for quality improvement and what the health plan does with the elements of its work that need improvement.

Although the process is new, HMO accreditation is fast becoming a condition of doing business. Only about 30 percent of HMOs have obtained the coveted accreditation status; many more will receive it in the next few years. It doesn't take that many Fortune 500 companies to demand accreditation before everybody starts to jump on board. How can an employer offer employees a health plan that is not accredited when there is an accreditation program available?

The first time an organization works through the accreditation process the complexity of the requirements is enormous. Some health plans do not get full accreditation on their first try, but this does not necessarily mean that they have lower quality than other plans.

Physician Credentialing

For years physicians have remained independent of accreditation procedures. If a physician passed the license examination and met the criteria of a hospital medical staff for admitting patients to the hospital, he or she was accepted as a health plan provider.

Managed care organizations now "credential" new physicians by checking their backgrounds and training. The credentialing process requires a whole series of steps including verification of background and training, verification of licenses and certifications, review of any malpractice cases, and a review of any sanctions placed upon the physician by Medicare or Medicaid.

But the credentialing process does not end there. For example, the National Committee for Quality Assurance suggests that physicians should be recredentialed every 24 months. This is done to keep current information about physicians. To qualify for recredentialing, physicians must submit to a thorough review of their practice patterns, the clinical outcomes they achieve, their continued compliance with utilization management policies, continuing education, maintenance of their valid license, and patient satisfaction survey results.

PROCESS MEASUREMENTS OF QUALITY

Measuring the process of quality means counting the number or percent of members who participate in appropriate care for their condition. We can say that a health plan has process quality if it is doing the things that are believed to result in positive health outcomes. Figure 19-3 lists some of the measures of process quality. Your health plan may not track all of the indicators of process quality. Managed care plans have just begun reporting on quality and you should not expect to see all these data from every plan.

By itself, measuring whether the health plan does the right things is still only part of the answer. The most important element of quality is what actually results from the process.

HEALTH OUTCOMES MEASUREMENTS OF QUALITY

Some patients are sicker than others when they see a physician. Either the disease affects them harder, they waited longer to seek care, or the disease is at a more advanced stage than for other patients with a similar diagnosis. Using a sophisticated method to account for how severe your illness is, known as a *severity of illness adjustment procedure,* the quality management staff compare the expected outcomes with the real outcomes.

As morbid as it sounds, how many people die within a given population (such as a health plan) is one of the traditional measures of outcome quality. When death rates are studied using a severity of illness adjustment procedure, death rates of patients with more severe illnesses are compared with death rates of similar patients. This is called a *severity adjusted mortality report.* Then when one health care organization can be compared with other organizations, it is compared on the basis of how severely ill the patients were when they were treated.

In addition to severity adjusted mortality reports, there are other mortality figures that are used to measure quality, such as neonatal mortality, general surgery mortality, heart surgery mortality, and heart attack mortality. Besides mor-

1. The percent of inpatients who are placed in a care mapping or critical pathway program
2. The percent of members who use the emergency room for care when they could have gone to their primary care clinic
3. The percent of high-risk patients who are placed in a case management program
4. The number of new members who make a visit to their primary care physician within sixty days of enrollment
5. The number of members with known medical conditions who attend self-care instruction programs
6. The number of cigarette smokers who attend health education programs
7. The percent of patients receiving colonoscopy and sigmoidoscopy screening according to industry-accepted guidelines
8. Timeliness of notifying patients of abnormal Pap smears
9. The percent of adults receiving cholesterol screening at least once every five years
10. The percent of women receiving Pap smear screening according to guidelines (once in a two-year period)
11. The percent of infants, children, and high-risk adults receiving recommended immunizations
12. The number of diabetic patients with evidence of semiannual physician visits
13. The number of cancellations of ambulatory procedure on the day of the procedure
14. The number of registered patients who leave the emergency room prior to completion of treatment
15. The number of unscheduled returns to the emergency room within 72 hours
16. The percent of members with advance directives
17. The percent of female members receiving mammograms according to guidelines
18. The percent of primary care physicians who participate in medical care evaluations each year
19. The percent of physicians who are evaluated on performance each year
20. The percent of female health plan members who receive prenatal care during the first trimester of pregnancy

FIGURE 19-3 Twenty measures of process quality.

tality rates, health care organizations monitor other outcome indicators, including the following:

1. The number of unscheduled readmissions to the hospital
2. The number of hospital-acquired infections
3. The percent of newborn babies with a birth weight of less than 2,500 grams
4. The number of suspected or confirmed adverse drug reactions

5. The percent of patients with skin pressure sores that develop after admission

6. The number of unscheduled returns to intensive care unit

Be aware that the information health plans study on quality should be gathered on large numbers of members. Only after many member's experiences are analyzed can appropriate conclusions be drawn. For instance, if only five patients receive a certain procedure and one dies, this is a 20 percent mortality rate—and may be pretty scary depending on the seriousness of the procedure. However, using information obtained from a small number of patients in the study may indicate an unusual event rather than an average.

Consumer Satisfaction

If HMO members are satisfied with the care that is provided, they get well faster and stay healthier longer. Consumer satisfaction is directly related to the degree of trust you have for your managed care team. When you trust your team to collaborate with you, you listen carefully to what the team members say. You are willing to endure a higher level of pain if it means you will get better faster. You take your situation seriously. You are willing to follow your physician's advice.

Health plans know that reports on consumer satisfaction, compared with other quality measures, are most often used by other consumers when judging a health plan's quality. Consumer satisfaction surveys are the best way to gauge how the whole organization or specific departments are performing.

Consumer satisfaction ratings commonly include the following types of measurements: overall satisfaction, quality of care, value, consumer service, access to specialists, and responsiveness.

Health Plan Performance and Cost Management

Employers are interested in health outcomes. They are also interested in the health plan's ability to control costs and to perform administratively. Here are some of the measures used to monitor performance:

1. Premium price trends (the annual increase or decrease in premium prices studied over time)

2. Utilization of inpatient care (inpatient days per 1,000 members)

3. Admissions per 1,000 members

4. Length of stay for various inpatient services such as obstetrics, intensive care, mental health, and medical-surgical

5. Savings generated based on medical necessity reviews (not paying providers for inappropriately billed charges)
6. Administrative costs per member per month
7. Turnaround time on claims processing (expressed in number of days)
8. Percent accuracy of claims processing
9. Health plan employee turnover rate

The HEDIS Program

In 1989 the National Committee for Quality Assurance (NCQA), the Washington, D.C. organization that accredits HMOs, began developing a uniform method of reporting quality to employer groups. The system that was developed is called HEDIS, the Health Plan Employer Data and Information Set. Several health plans are developing their own system for reporting on quality, but HEDIS is becoming the most popular and is likely to become the standard that other reporting systems follow.

HEDIS reports are a cluster of quality measures including preventive services offered to HMO members, prenatal care, services provided for members with chronic illnesses, access to care, and member satisfaction. HEDIS reporting systems allow the NCQA to take its monitoring function one step further by actually reporting specific quality indicators to consumers. The HEDIS system, though still being refined and improved, provides companies a way to compare one health plan with another.

Report Cards Refined and Expanded

Under pressure from the large employer groups, some HMOs are now gathering and reporting quality on their own. U.S. Health Care of Pennsylvania, United Health Care Corporation in Minnesota, and Kaiser Permanente of Northern California published report cards for the general public while dozens of other HMOs are gathering the information and making it available to employers on demand. Meanwhile these report cards are being refined to be more understandable to the general public, and experiments are underway to develop simplified star rating systems.

Report cards for health plans are now being used by PPOs, too. Ethix Corporation, a five million member PPO with provider networks in Denver, Minneapolis, and Philadelphia, published its own quality report card in 1994. Similar to what HMOs are doing, Ethix uses guidelines provided by the NCQA. Other PPOs are expected to start reporting on quality as employer demand for report cards increases.

Health plan reputations are no better than the reputations of their physicians.

Some are developing report cards on their primary care physicians. But managed care organizations are taking this concept one step further by linking physician payment to quality of care. These quality-based payment programs for both physicians and hospital providers are well received by those who understand the importance of quality improvement.

CONCLUSION

Not all individuals interested in enrolling in an HMO will concern themselves with reading and understanding reports on quality. Some consumers who are thinking of enrolling in a health plan simply want to know that satisfied members are having good experiences with the organization. Others prefer to depend upon the advice of their physician. And others may have little choice if their employer selects a health plan for them. Regardles of the degree of choice you have, it pays to become more informed about the quality of your managed care plan.

CHAPTER 20

A Look to the Future

The year is 2020. You are on a trip from your home in Detroit passing through Cheyenne, Wyoming, when you get seriously ill. Upon arriving at the local hospital emergency room your family gives introductory information to the registration clerk who, in turn, places a scanning device over your left shoulder where an implanted memory device contains all your relevant medical information. Within seconds your medical history is beamed into view for the attending physician. If you have written any advance directives, a copy of these and other important documents will be available for the emergency room physician to view.

If the case is serious, a phone call is made to your family physician back home who, from the convenience of his or her home, office, or hospital, is linked via satellite or telephone line for an instant consultation with you and the ER physician. Your family physician actually sees a live video of you on a computer screen along with a summary of the emergency room physician's diagnosis. You are able to see and talk to your physician.

WHAT THE COMMUNICATION SYSTEM COULD LOOK LIKE

In the future all these things and more can happen within minutes of your arrival at a hospital. You will have the peace of mind that your family physician will know everything that is going on and can give instant advice to a physician who has never seen you before. Tests will not have to be duplicated, for as soon as any procedures are completed at the hospital, a copy of your medical records will be sent by computer back to your physician's records for follow-up care as soon as you arrive home. In fact, by the time you arrive home you will have an appointment set up in advance to see your physician. The Cheyenne hospital business office will send an invoice to your health plan which will, in turn, give another computer command to transfer funds from its account to the bank account of the integrated network to which the Cheyenne hospital and emergency room physician belongs.

If your case is particularly unusual or enlightening about any common illnesses, a summary of your case, with your consent and without the personal information about you, will be placed automatically on the Wyoming statewide medical education computer bulletin board for physicians in training at any Wyoming hospital. The next morning during "computer grand rounds" at the teaching hospitals in the state the emergency room physician will present your case in dialogue with the physicians in training. Other physicians will have an opportunity to ask questions of the attending physician. In this way, young physicians in training can gain the experience of seeing a complete process of care and medical outcomes.

When you get home to Detroit, several messages will be waiting in your personal computer E-mail box. One will be a patient satisfaction survey form that you will be asked to complete and send back by computer to your health plan and to the hospital in Wyoming. Another may be a note from a physician in training asking if you care to comment on the outcomes of your treatment plan. A third will be personal instructions written by the treatment team involved in your care while you were in Wyoming. The emergency room nurse, physician, and your own personal physician will all have advice on how you should manage your health in the future.

Does this sound too outrageous? With the technology we have available, this is possible now. And, it will not be too many more years before the communication systems are in place to do this and much more.

When you sign up with a health plan or change HMOs during open enrollment, your name and medical history will be loaded into the health plan's computer system. If you do not have a medical history on record, you will be encouraged to visit a primary care physician for a physical examination and medical history. The information gathered during this visit will be loaded into the computer system of both the physician's office and the health plan. The information will also be available on line to other health care providers who are expected to render care should you get sick and need their services. Reasonable protocols for information security will be used to preserve confidentiality of information about you.

After the data is loaded into the computer system, the computer will analyze the information and make specific recommendations to your physician based on the experience of thousands of people with similar circumstances. Your physician or nurse will probably contact you following the analysis of your medical record. They will give you a verbal and written report of what the physician recommends to maintain and improve your health. If you make contact with a physician, an emergency room, or some other provider who is linked with the health plan's computer system, the transaction will be added to the computer medical record.

All this is done to maintain access to care, continuity of care, and access to care, and to improve the ability of physicians and nurses to prescribe the most appropriate levels of care.

In the future, computer records of hundreds of patients will be analyzed to assist the health plan and its physicians in improving clinical services, making their scheduling policies more efficient. As the number of computer records grows from the care given to thousands of health plan members, health plan researchers will monitor the performance of physicians and nurses. Managers will be able to judge the treatment effectiveness of 90 to 95 percent of the services provided. As a result, the "intelligence" of the computer will reflect the additional learning that occurs with this research. It will also assist the health plan in analyzing how much of the premium dollars it spends to provide the care you need.

When you are admitted to the hospital in the future, several departments will be given information about your case to assist them in ordering supplies and preparing for procedures that the physician is expected to order. This information, along with information from all the other patients admitted to the hospital, will help the hospital management adjust the number of nurses and other workers to meet the changing demand. If your case requires a more intense level of care than other patients with similar diagnoses, this information will be noted in the computer. The computer will automatically send messages to the nursing unit and to the physician reminding these individuals about any special needs you have. A personalized care plan generated by the computer will give nurses and physicians a guide of what to expect during your stay in the hospital. You or your family will be informed regarding the expected outcomes of hospital care.

When you are discharged from the hospital more computer analysis will be completed as researchers study the effectiveness of care you received. The computer data will be collected from other patients for studying the effectiveness of hospital work units. If you complete a patient satisfaction survey, your responses will automatically be grouped with surveys of other patients. This retrospective review will be conducted entirely by the use of computer information. The computer will also generate a customized checklist of things that you should do following inpatient care. The same computer will generate a list of things that your primary care physician and nurse should do to follow up your hospital stay, such as suggesting when you should visit your physician again.

INTERACTIVE VIDEO AND BIOTECHNOLOGY

One of the persistent problems we now face in health care will be solved in the next quarter century: getting information to you about health topics when you want it. Mary Gardiner-Jones, president of the Washington, D.C.-based Consumer Interest Research Institute, sees interactive video technology available in every home within the next 25 years. Interactive video offers, in her view, innovative ways to redefine how we learn, how to teach people, and how to motivate others to act for their own good. This will take a central role in health care system of the future.

As consumers learn to take more responsibility for their own health, more self-help groups will develop around the interactive video technology. In this way, even people living in rural, isolated communities will be able to connect with others who have similar health interests in a manner that is much more convenient than driving or flying.

Other visionaries agree with Mary Gardiner-Jones. Russell Coile Jr., president of the Santa Clarita, California, Health Forecasting Group, believes that by the year 2020 many people will have personal interactive communication devices in their home where they will be on line with their health plans. "Let's assume, for example," Coile says, "that you have a chronic condition. You will be on line to your care managers checking in once each day or once a week or as often as necessary." The personal communication device will include a television camera which transmits real-time video of you directly to your physician while you are having a conversation with him or her. Many routine physician's appointments in the future may involve sitting in the family room while having a fifteen-minute interview with your physician.

Clement Bezold of the Institute for Alternative Futures in Virginia reports that technology already exists that can be placed in the home for what he calls biomonitoring. For example, you will have the ability right in your own home to monitor your own condition and then relay this information directly to your managed care team. You may even carry a device with you—in the form of a wristwatch, eyeglasses, or even something as small as an earring—that will monitor such things as blood pressure, blood flow and blood chemistry, and the body electrical system. Such a device will have a transmitter that can relay the information to the physician.

You are probably familiar with X-ray machines, CT "CAT" scanners, and MRI scanners that have been used for many years to take pictures of internal body structures. In the future we will have scanning devices that will scan either the entire body or body parts for signs of disease. A new type of scanner is being developed that will monitor and report on the functioning of body systems. Clement Bezold believes that within 25 years we will have scanning devices, similar to airport security scanners, that you will simply walk through and they will capture vital information that can be relayed to your physician. The technology will become so sensitive that to have a checkup you will not need to visit a primary care provider. All you will need to do is walk through a scanner that may be located in a convenient shopping location or at work, swipe your health plan card through a machine that will verify your eligibility for services, and then transmit your information to your physician.

HOSPITALS IN 2020

The number of hospitals and hospital beds in America has been on the decline for the last 15 years. This trend will continue through the year 2000. Even the large tertiary research/teaching hospitals will be smaller. There will be less duplication of services within a community as hospitals work cooperatively with health plans and medical groups to eliminate redundant technology and services.

The hospitals of the future will remain the typical place where people go when they need 24-hour observation after surgery, when they have a serious disease, or after experiencing trauma. New hospitals built after 1995 will have different internal designs than existing hospitals because they will be configured for short stays, with less distinction between inpatient and outpatient facilities. Hospitals will still have surgery suites, intensive care units, and maternity departments. But many patients who stay overnight in the hospital now will be able to go home at night and return to the hospital for treatment during the daytime. Fewer and fewer traditional hospital beds will be needed. Hospital rooms will be larger and equipped to accommodate family members who want to stay with ill family members.

Instead of the hospital being the center of the health care community, in the future it will simply be one of dozens of ways care can be given. Hospitals will become an intermediate step in the process of care.

HEALTH CARE PERSONNEL

Physicians have begun to realize how much they will have to change in the future as more managed care principles are used in America. Now there are two specialists for every one primary care physician. However, in the future the ratio will begin to approach one specialist for every one or two primary care physicians.

Primary care physicians now enjoy the spotlight as the co-captains of the managed care team. In the long-term future, however, primary care will be provided by many more nonphysicians than physicians. Nurses, physician assistants, and others will be independent community care workers who will provide much of the basic care for which people now turn to physicians.

This will no doubt be true for certain specialty services now regarded as the sole domain of the physician. For example, futurists see cardiology nurses, orthopedic practitioners, and diabetes specialists working independently of physicians to care for patients with chronic conditions needing frequent contact with health care providers.

Training of health care professionals will change drastically in the future. Clement Bezold sees the use of sophisticated simulation devices for training physicians and nurses. Computers and synthetic materials will be used to create the virtual patient. Physicians of all specialties can learn how to diagnose disease and how to monitor the progress of a patient under treatment all on computer. Using virtual reality technology surgeons in training will have the chance to practice surgery in the nonsterile atmosphere of a surgery simulator. Surgeons who perform highly specialized procedures will have opportunities to keep their skills at a high level by using simulators. But these same technologies will allow nurses and/or consumers to do more of the work of a primary care physician or specialist.

HEALTH PROMOTION

Once the utilization of services for those who are ill is refined and refined again for the optimal use of resources that will generate the best clinical results, what is left? Russell Coile says it is health promotion. In the future, health care professionals will understand far better than they do today the elements that promote health and prevent disease. Clement Bezold believes that we will better understand the behavioral contributors to health. Information about your health behavior, illnesses or conditions, and genetic predispositions toward certain illnesses will all be kept in an information system by managed care providers that will enable them to predict, prevent, and manage.

Joe Zupec, vice president of Health Plan Management Services in Atlanta, also sees accountability for health outcomes broadening in the future. In five to ten years health plans will be able to show how quality is managed in specific situations, and in the distant future this accountability will broaden to include whole populations served by the health plans. Zupec says that we will examine an entire group of people who have joined managed care organizations and analyze what happened to this group over a period of time based upon their state of health when they enrolled and their state of health later.

But there are two sides to the coins spent on health care when it comes to responsibility for promoting good health. If managed care plans are held increasingly responsible for doing all they can to prevent disease, then members will be held to a higher standard of personal behavior, which will have a direct affect on preventing disease. Dr. Richard Hart, dean of the Loma Linda University School of Public Health in California, believes that increasing financial incentives will be offered to those who engage in lifestyles conducive to staying healthy. And, for those who continue to engage in self-destructive behavior, health plans will eventually ask them to change their behavior because if they do not these plans will take less responsibility for their care.

Dr. Hart believes that the reality of implementing this type of policy will be relatively easy for some segments of the population and more difficult for others. Some individuals because of the environment in which they were raised learned to cope with the rest of society through self-destructive behaviors. The result is that the rest of society will continue, as it does now, to spend a large proportion of health care resources for treatment of these largely preventible conditions. The political battles that rage over designing such a policy will, no doubt, be intense as we move through the next quarter century.

It seems clear that one trend will continue: Health systems will be required by employers and government to actively work as a health system instead of an illness treatment system. Margaret O'Kane says that health plans will help members maximize their health "rather than waiting until diseases have caused so much destruction that the health care system needs to come in with its tertiary care."

STRUCTURE OF THE MANAGED CARE
INDUSTRY IN THE FUTURE

"If you look at the fundamental product in the future," says Clement Bezold, "managed care will be a partnership with their customers to not do what they do now, which is manage symptoms and acute presentations of illness, but actually manage health." The distinctions between who provides care will blur. Managed care organizations will work closely with community members in defining the specifications of the health care system. Community governance of the health plan, similar to the system used by the Group Health Cooperative of Puget Sound, will become the norm.

Russell Coile Jr. sees the managed care industry of the future as a seamless system of care. It will include health care delivered at the workplace either as an on-site clinic or as a mobile clinic traveling from company to company. Interactive video technology will be available for employees at the work site so they can check in with their managed care team there, if necessary. A similar arrangement will likely be available at schools and colleges. Further consolidation will be the rule for the future as managed care networks become more fully able to provide care both in your own community and in major cities to which you may travel.

According to Coile, the ideal managed care organization of the future will provide a comprehensive range of services in a coordinated pattern of care with a degree of complexity and care management that is not seen today. Today's consumers must be much more aware of how the system works. They must actively interact with their managed care plans to get the system to work for themselves.

In the year 2020, managed care will be almost hassle-free. That does not mean that consumers will no longer have any say in their health care decisions. On the contrary, consumers will be more actively involved in the management of their care. It means that the various providers will be closely interconnected through common goals, training, and information systems that the consumer will be able to be a more informed manager of care.

Michael Weinstein, president of Managed Care Planning Associates in Encino, California, believes that we will see tremendous consolidation in the health care industry. He says:

> Health plan members will have a limited choice from among only five to ten health plans that serve the national market. The outcome quality will be known about these plans. They will be compared to national standards for quality and the public will know what kind of health care they are receiving. The information will be specific to each physician, hospital, home care agency, surgery center, skilled nursing facility, and health plan in each city.

Mary Gardiner-Jones and Jane Preston, M.D., president of the American Telemedicine Association, both see our homes as the primary locations for health care delivery in the year 2020. Health care workers will be available at clinics, physician's offices, and hospitals, but they will also visit homes of patients to whom they are assigned by managed care teams. And when home visitation is not possible because of logistical challenges, interactive computer communication devices will link patients in their homes to their care givers.

Closer relationships will exist between health plans and suppliers of medical products such as medicine. Shared information systems between the business partners will assist medical researchers to develop new medicines faster.

CONSUMER ATTITUDES AND BEHAVIORS

As managed care networks continue to consolidate or merge with other networks, consumers will be less likely to change health plans as often as they change them now. And now there are hundreds of choices for basic health coverage, but if the experts are right, there will be fewer organizations from which to choose in the future.

SELF CARE WILL BECOME DOMINANT

Most of the experts agree that in the future self care will play a much more dominant role in managing health than it does now. The challenge will be to incorpo-

rate more self care into the mainstream of health care delivery. Alternative therapies, now considered on the fringes of medicine, will become commonly
accepted.

With access to personal medical devices and assisted by the latest in communication technology, you can actually do more diagnosis and treatment right
from your own home. Acting with guidance from your managed care team,
you will have instant access to information that will help you determine whether
the symptoms you experienced this morning are serious and need immediate
medical attention or whether you should just lay low for the day and monitor
yourself.

The practice guidelines being developed now in most managed care environ-
ments will become available to selected groups of patients who have been diagnosed as having a chronic disease. You will, for example, be able to access specific
information about what to do if your blood pressure goes above a certain level at
the same time that a blood test, administered at home, indicates a problem. When
you access the guideline using your personal communication device, your medical record will be automatically updated and a message is passed to your primary
care physician. If the situation is urgent, you will be automatically linked to a live
person who can immediately advise you whether to go to the health plan clinic
for care or whether to get a prescription for medicine, which can be automatically
transmitted to the pharmacy for delivery within the hour.

Will all this technology reduce or eliminate the need for personal contact with
highly trained medical personnel? The answer is absolutely not.

THE HUMAN SIDE OF CARE

William Osheroff, M.D., medical director of Pacificare Health System in Cypress,
California, reminds us that the human side of medicine will be needed just as
much in the future as it is today. "We have come from a system of paternalism,"
Dr. Osheroff says, "where the physician says 'this is what you need' and the patient goes along with it. In a few years we are going to have a population who are
much more involved in their medical decisions. There will be electronic interactive media for patients to use in their home for home care."

Dr. Osheroff suggests that by the advances of science we have a tendency
to get beyond our own humanness. It is true that consumers will be more involved in the diagnosis and treatment of their own illnesses. But there is a humanness about us that requires real contact with others, that requires care
and understanding, support and sharing. Technology, per se, does not satisfy
these human needs. Much of the medical care delivered today is primary care,
time spent attending to the human needs of people, not simply the biomedical
needs.

Finally, the ability to make sound judgments regarding patient health care can come only from an experienced family physician who has worked closely with patients over a period of time. We will never just sit down in front of a computer, type in the word "headache," and expect the computer to respond in a way that treats the whole person. Only a human being can do that. So, even though consumers will know more about caring for themselves and have technological wizardry at their fingertips, there will always be a need for experienced physicians to guide and manage their care.

Glossary of Terms

accreditation   A judgment made by a professional society or other recognized organization that a health care provider substantially meets the appropriate standards of care. An *accreditation agency* is an independent organization that answers to a trade association or a group made up of consumers and providers.

accreditation survey   The process of evaluating a health services organization to determine whether or not accreditation will be awarded.

adverse selection   The enrollment of higher than average numbers of high-risk or unhealthy members into a managed care organization. Adverse selection causes higher than average costs. See also *favorable selection.*

ancillary services   Support services that are sometimes needed for diagnosis or treatment. Examples of ancillary services include X ray, CT scanning, MRI scanning, ultrasound, treadmill testing, pulmonary function testing, physical therapy, speech therapy, occupational therapy, medical laboratory services, and colonoscopy. These services must be ordered by the physician before they can be provided for you.

authorization   The process used by managed care organizations to respond to requests for services not performed by primary care physicians.

benefit agreement   Sometimes called a *subscriber agreement, member agreement, benefit package,* or *benefit plan,* this is the written contract specifying which health services are provided by your health plan. When you sign up with a managed care organization you agree to pay for these specifically defined services. The health plan is obligated to provide only those services listed in the benefit agreement. If you want services not listed in the benefit agreement, you usually have to pay for them out of your own money.

board certification   A status awarded by a professional association indicating that the health care practitioner has met specific standards of knowledge and clinical skill within a specified field. The board certification process usually involves passing a written and oral examination administered by the professional certification committee.

board eligible   A status awarded by a professional medical or surgical association indicating that the health care practitioner has successfully completed an accredited residency training program. It means that the healthcare practitioner is qualified to take the board certification examination within a specified time period. If the examination is not taken and passed within the specific time period, board eligibility status is usually withdrawn.

capitation   A monthly fixed payment to your health care provider regardless of how much care is provided. This payment is usually set as a per member per month (PMPM) dollar amount. Capitation payments for different medical and surgical specialties vary widely.

claim   A formal request by a health care provider to receive payment for services provided to you. Claims are submitted in writing. The trend, however, is to maintain computer links between providers and health plans so that claims can be submitted electronically.

closed panel   A panel or group of physicians under contract with or employed by an HMO to provide health services exclusively to that HMO's members. The closed panel of doctors work in the HMO-owned clinic or health center. See also *staff model* and *group model*.

continuous quality improvement (CQI)   The management process where health care providers evaluate and modify healthcare services for the purpose of improving quality. This is sometimes called *total quality management* or *TQM*.

copayment   Your share of the cost of care. In managed care systems this is often a set amount. For example, your copayments may be $10 per doctor visit, $5 per prescription, and so forth. Most HMOs require members to pay modest copayments when they receive care. You should pay your copayment at the time you visit the doctor or purchase your medication. Read your benefit agreement to find out what copayments are required. Sometimes this information is printed on your membership card.

CQI   See *continuous quality improvement*.

credentialing process/standards   The process of evaluating a healthcare provider to determine whether the provider meets certain standards of knowledge and clinical skill. The process also involves the granting or denial of privileges to perform specific services or treatments within defined limits. Credentials are evaluated based on the professional's formal educational training, state licensure, post graduate continuing education training, and clinical experience. During the process of credentialing the credentialing committee of the health care organization will evaluate known problems, such as medical malpractice suits and judgments and official disciplinary actions.

deductible   A fixed dollar amount that you have to pay before your health plan will reimburse your doctor or hospital. Traditional health insurance usually requires you to pay a yearly deductible. However, in many HMOs there are no deductibles required.

direct contracting   Occurs when an individual or an employer contracts directly with those who provide the health care services without going through a health plan. Direct contracting allows an employer to customize a benefit agreement for the specific group of employees who are covered.

discounted fee-for-service   Similar to *fee-for-service* except that your health plan negotiates a discount off your doctor's usual and customary fees. This is an advantage to your health plan. However, it may not mean that you will pay a discounted copayment.

dual choice   A choice allowed by an employer when you select a health care plan permitting you to choose from among at least two alternatives with one alternative being an HMO.

elective surgery   A surgical procedure that may be desired by the health plan member but is not necessarily mandatory for improving health or quality of life.

eligibility verification   The process of confirming that you are a subscriber to the health plan. In some plans this also means confirming what level of services you are entitled to and what financial obligations you are responsible for at the time you receive services.

enrollment   The process of selecting and signing up as a member of a managed care organization. See also *open enrollment.*

EPO   See *exclusive provider organization.*

exclusive provider organization (EPO)   The type of relationship between your HMO and your doctor where the doctor gets paid on a negotiated amount (under written agreement) and you are required to use this doctor exclusively unless you want to pay for the cost of care out of your own pocket. Using the EPO doctors and hospitals usually means that your HMO will pay for a larger proportion of the cost.

false negative   Medical test results showing that a person may be healthy when they are not healthy.

false positive   Medical test results showing that a person may be ill when they are not ill.

favorable selection   The enrollment of higher than average number of low-risk or healthy members into a managed care organization. Favorable selection causes lower than average costs. See also *adverse selection.*

fee-for-service   The traditional way to pay for medical care. When the doctor or hospital provides you with a specific service, you or your health plan pay for that service at the doctor's or hospital's usual and customary fees. See also *discounted fee-for-service.*

formulary   The list of prescription medications that may be used without authorization. The formulary is selected based on effectiveness of the drug as well as the cost of the drug. Certain specialized, high-cost medications may be required for treatment but are left off the formulary because the managed care organization wants the provider to obtain authorization to prescribe the medicine. In these cases, authorization is given unless an alternative medicine that is just as effective can be identified.

gatekeeper   The physician who has primary responsibility to manage your medical care. The gatekeeper physician must be knowledgeable about a wide range of medical and surgical issues. If the gatekeeper determines that you may have a serious illness needing the care of a specialist, he or she has the responsibility to get authorization from the HMO to refer you to a specialist for care. Usually the gatekeeper physician is a family doctor, a pediatrician, or a general internist. In some organizations obstetrician-gynecologists are also considered gatekeepers.

group model   A type of HMO where the health plan contracts with an organized multispecialty medical group to provide physician services to members. One type of group, closed panel, is the group that has been formed by the HMO and that works in the HMO-owned facilities for the sole purpose of serving that HMO's members. The other type of group, the open panel, is independent and maintains the freedom to contract with more than one HMO to serve a variety of health plan members.

HCFA   See *health care financing administration.*

Health Care Financing Administration (HCFA)   A division of the United States Department of Health and Human Services, HCFA is the contracting agency for HMOs that provide services to Medicare beneficiaries.

health maintenance organization (HMO)   One of the types of managed care organizations. This is a health plan that provides both the payment for your care as well as the actual delivery of the care. The HMO agrees to provide a comprehensive set of benefits in return for a fixed, monthly payment per person. You may be required to pay a small *copayment,* but usually no additional fees are required.

HMO   See *health maintenance organization.*

home care   Nursing care that is provided to you when you are living at your own residence.

house staff   Graduates of medical school who are appointed to a hospital specialty training program. House staff physicians participate in patient care under the direction of licensed independent doctors.

indemnity health plan   The traditional health insurance plan that allows you to choose any doctor or hospital you need at any time for any type of medical or surgical care. Under indemnity insurance you have a greater degree of control over utilization than in managed care organizations. Most indemnity health plans require you to pay a small percentage (between 10 and 30 percent) of the cost of your care.

independent practice association (IPA)   Sometimes called the independent physician association or individual practice association, the IPA is a collection of physicians who have banded together for the purpose of contracting with one or more managed care organizations. Each of the physicians in the IPA maintain separate private practice offices to treat other patients. Sometimes the IPA is responsible for the financial management of HMO contracts with the physicians, utilization management, claims processing, and other services required to serve the members of a managed care organization.

intern   A graduate of a medical school who works in a hospital for a specific period of time until he or she decides upon a medical or surgical specialty. An intern is sometimes not licensed by the state to practice medicine since he or she does not take the license examination until after the internship.

IPA   See *independent practice association.*

IPA model HMO   An HMO that contracts with one or more IPAs to provide medical services to HMO members. See also *IPA.*

JCAHO   See *Joint Commission on the Accreditation of Health Care Organizations.*

Joint Commission on the Accreditation of Health Care Organizations (JCAHO)
An accrediting body that evaluates and awards accreditation status to facilities such as hospitals, skilled nursing facilities, and health maintenance organizations.

managed care   Any system of care that attempts to control your health care costs, improve your access to care, improve the appropriateness of care for your condition, coordinate your care, and monitor the use of care. Most health plans use the principles of managed care to some degree. HMOs are known for using all of the managed care techniques.

managed care organization   Any organization that uses the principles of managed care as an integral part of doing business. See also *HMO, PPO,* and *managed care.*

medical group   An organized collection of physicians who have a common business interest through a partnership or some form of shared ownership. Some medical groups are comprised of physicians representing a single specialty. Other groups are made up of physicians from two or more specialties. See also *multispecialty group.*

medical record   A written or electronic account of your medical history, current illness, diagnosis, details of treatments, and chronological notes on the progress you make toward healing or recovery. This is a legal document that you are entitled to read. Your medical record is said to be "complete" when it contains all of the above information as well as a description of your condition when you are discharged from the hospital. Completeness also means that the documents your record contains have been authenticated by your physician's signature. The medical record must be legible. There are strict rules regarding the confidentiality of the medical record.

medical student   An individual who is in a university medical education program but who has not completed that course of study. The first two years of medical school are spent in the university classroom and laboratories learning medical science. In the third and fourth years medical students spend much of their time in hospitals learning the practical side of medicine.

Medigap insurance   A health insurance program in which you pay a monthly premium to receive health benefits that cover what your main health plan does not cover. Popular among people who are on Medicare, the Medigap insurance pays for most if not all the deductibles and copayments required by Medicare.

member   Sometimes called a subscriber, beneficiary, enrollee, or covered subscriber, the HMO member is the person for whom care is provided under the benefit agreement.

multispecialty group   A type of medical group comprised of several medical and surgical specialists working together and sharing ownership. This is a popular type of group that HMOs prefer to contract with for services.

National Committee for Quality Assurance (NCQA) An accrediting body that surveys managed care organizations to determine whether these organizations meet agreed upon standards of quality.

NCQA See *National Committee for Quality Assurance.*

network model A type of HMO that contracts with a variety of medical groups to serve some geographic area. A variety of choices from among medical groups and IPAs is sometimes desired by employers.

open enrollment The time period when you are given the chance to change your health plan. Open enrollment usually occurs once each year for a period of fifteen or thirty days. While required to offer open enrollment at least once each year for Medicare beneficiaries, some HMOs for seniors offer open enrollment all year long.

open panel A type of medical group that contracts with more than one HMO. See also *group model.*

outcome The results of health care services being performed. Outcomes include clinical, measurable indicators of health status. They also include your opinions about the process of care as well as the professional opinions of your managed care team members.

out of network A physician, hospital, or other health care provider who is not under contract with the HMO to provide services to that HMO's members. By receiving care from an out-of-network provider the member often must pay a higher deductible or copayment or both.

peer review The evaluation of the clinical practice activities as well as the clinical outcomes of one health care professional (usually a physician) by others of the same specialty and geographic region.

per member per month (PMPM) The method by which most managed care organizations account for revenue and expenses.

PMPM See *per member per month.*

point-of-service plan (POS) Sometimes called an "open-ended HMO," the point-of-service plan offers the major benefits of both HMOs and PPOs. Members have more choice of providers and the HMO retains strict control over utilization. This type of plan is usually an option to a regular HMO program. As a member of this type of plan, you can use services of physicians not under contract with the HMO. In exchange for this added choice, you usually pay a higher deductible and higher copayments.

POS See *point-of-service plan.*

PPO See *preferred provider organization.*

preferred provider organization (PPO) A managed care system under which your traditional health insurance company contracts with several physicians and hospitals. The physicians and hospitals who sign up with the PPO agree to be paid a discounted fee-for-service. If you have a PPO health plan, you will probably pay deductibles and copayments.

If you do not use the healthcare providers listed with the PPO, you will have reduced benefits or have to pay a higher deductible and copayment.

prepaid health plan   Another term for a health maintenance organization that prepays the doctor or hospital for your care each month whether you need care or not. See also *capitation.*

prepaid medical group   The early form of HMO, this is an organized group of physicians who agree to provide a comprehensive set of physician services for a negotiated, prepaid amount of money for each member each month. See also *prepaid health plan* and *capitation.*

primary care physician   A physician trained in one or more of the following areas: family medicine, general practice, general internal medicine, pediatric medicine. Some health plans include obstetrics-gynecology as one of the types of primary care physicians.

private practice   The traditional arrangement for physicians who wanted to care for a variety of patients. Physicians in private practice provide services in exchange for fees paid by you or your health plan. See also *fee-for-service.*

providers   A broad term referring to the licensed or certified health care professionals and organizations that provide care to HMO members. Providers can be independent professionals in private practice or they can be members of an organized group, such as a multispecialty medical group. Common providers in managed care include hospitals, medical groups, home care companies, skilled nursing facilities, medical equipment companies, primary care physicians, and specialist physicians. In managed care, providers have a close working relationship with an HMO either as an employee, a contracted professional, or an HMO-owned facility such as an hospital or clinic.

resident   A physician who is in a formal hospital training program. A resident physician focuses his or her learning on a recognized medical or surgical specialty. Many resident physicians are licensed after they complete their internship year. After successfully completing an accredited residency program, the physician is considered board eligible, meaning that he or she is qualified to take the board certification examination for the chosen specialty.

service area   Sometimes called "catchment area" or "enrollment area," this is the geographical area that the HMO serves. A service area can be primary or secondary. A primary service area is the clearly defined region where most of the HMO members come from and where most, if not all, of the health care providers are located.

staff model HMO   An HMO that directly employs all the health care professionals, including physicians, on a salary basis. Your staff model HMO probably owns its own clinics and may even own or manage the HMO hospital.

supplemental insurance   See *Medigap insurance.*

third-party administrator (TPA)   An organization that specializes in processing claims for care by collecting premiums and authorizing payment for services that the physician or hospital provides to you. Sometimes these types of organizations provide other related services such as utilization review, member services, and physician contracting.

total quality management (TQM)   See *continuous quality improvement.*

TPA   See *third-party administrator.*

utilization   How much and how often you use medical services that are covered benefits. In managed care organizations, utilization is carefully monitored for appropriateness, cost, and treatment effectiveness. Managed care organizations do not want you to use the health system inappropriately by getting less care than you need or by getting more care than is medically necessary to achieve desired results.

utilization management   Sometimes called utilization review, this is the process of monitoring and controlling the utilization of services by each health plan member. See also *utilization.*

utilization review   See *utilization management.*

APPENDIX II

Where to Get More Information on Managed Care

1. United States government

U.S. Department of Health and Human Services
Agency for Health Care Policy and Research
Health Care Financing Administration
Office of Prepaid Health Care

2. Your state department of insurance or department of corporations

Check your telephone book or call your
state information phone line to get the
phone number.

3. Professional and trade associations

American Association of Preferred
  Provider Organizations (PPOs)
1101 Connecticut Avenue NW, #700
Washington, DC 20036
202-429-5133

American Group Practice Association
  (Medical groups serving managed care
  plans)
1422 Duke Street
Alexandria, VA 22314
703-838-0033

American Managed Care & Review
  Association (industry trade association
  of HMOs and related organizations)
1200 19th Street NW, #200
Washington, DC 20036-2437
202-728-0506

American Telemedicine Association
  (promotes the development of
  telemedicine)
1 American Center
600 Congress Avenue, #1750
Austin, TX 78701
512-476-2307

Group Health Association of America
  (HMO industry trade association)
1129 20th Street NW, #600
Washington DC 20036
202-778-3268

Health Insurance Association of America
  (Health insurance industry trade
  association)
Managed Care Division
1025 Connecticut Avenue NW
Washington, DC 20036
202-223-7780

Managed Health Care Association
  (Coalition of HMOs and employer
  groups that want to improve quality of
  care)
1225 I Street NW, #300
Washington, DC 20005
202-371-8232

Medical Group Management Association
  (Medical groups that serve managed
  care plans)
104 Inverness Terrace East
Englewood, CO 80112
303-799-1111

National Association of Managed Care
  Physicians
4435 Waterfront Drive, #101
Glen Allen, VA 23058-4765
804-527-1905

National Business Coalition on Health
  (Constituents include regional and
  local business coalitions on health care
  cost containment)
1015 18th Street NW, #450
Washington DC 20036
202-775-9300

5. Accreditation bodies for managed care organizations

American Accreditation Program, Inc.
  (PPOs)
9944 Lawyers Road
Vienna, VA 22181
703-255-1200

Joint Commission on the Accreditation of
  Health Care Organizations (JCAHO)
  (Hospitals and Health Delivery Systems)
One Renaissance Bl
Oakbrook Terrace, IL 60181
708-916-5600

National Committee on Quality
  Assurance (HMOs)
1350 New York Avenue, #700
Washington, DC 20005
202-628-5788

6. Consumer information resources

Consumer Health Information Research
  Institute
(Publications on how to be a better
  educated health care consumer)
300 E. Pink Hill Road
Independence, MO 64057-3220
816-228-4595

Insurance Information Institute
800-331-9146

National Insurance Consumer Help line
800-942-4242

National Insurance Consumer
  Organization
(Ask for the "Buyer's Guide to Insurance")
121 N. Payne Street
Alexandria, VA 22314
703-549-8050

Public Citizen Health Research (Health
  care industry watch-dog group)
2000 P Street NW
Washington, DC 20036
202-833-3000

Weiss Research, Inc. (Ratings on HMOs
  and other health insurance companies)
P.O. Box 2923
West Palm Beach, FL 33402-2923
407-684-8100
800-289-9222

7. Other organizations

Foundation for Informed Medical
  Decision-making
7251 Strasenburgh
Hanover, NY 03755-3863
603-650-1180

Health Outcomes Institute
2001 Killebrew Drive, #122
Bloomington, MN 55425
612-858-9188

Institute for Alternative Futures
108 N. Alfred Street
Alexandria, VA 22314
703-684-5880

Rand Corporation
1700 Main Street
Santa Monica, CA 90406
310-393-0411

Bibliography

AARP. "Choosing an HMO: An evaluation checklist," *American Association of Retired Persons,* Health Advocacy Services Program Department, Washington, DC, 1986.

Agency for Healthcare Policy and Research, *Diagnosing and managing unstable angina,* U.S. Department of Health and Human Services, Public Health Service, Washington, D.C., March 1994.

"Are HMOs the answer?" *Consumer Reports,* vol. 57, no. 8, August 1992, pp. 519–521.

Ballard ML, Terze MM. "Automated credentialing: A practical approach to quality measurement," *AAPPO Journal,* American Association of Preferred Provider Organizations, June/July 1993, pp. 10–13, 36.

Barlow J. "Practice parameters and outcomes measurement: Managing for quality," *Medical Group Management Journal,* January/February 1994, pp. 12–17.

Barsky AJ. "The paradox of health," *The New England Journal of Medicine,* February 18, 1988, pp. 414–418.

Battagliola M. "Making employees better health care consumers," *Business & Health,* June 1992, pp. 22–28.

Bernstein SJ, Hilborne LH. "Clinical indicators: The road to quality care?" *The Joint Commission Journal on Quality Improvement,* November 1993, pp. 501–509.

Boland P. *Making managed healthcare work: A practical guide to strategies and solutions,* Aspen Publishing, Inc., Gaithersburg, MD, 1993.

Bradbury RC, Golec JH, Stearns FE. "Comparing low-severity hospital admissions in IPA HMOs and indemnity-type programs," *Hospital & Health Services Administration,* Spring 1993, pp. 45–61.

Braus P. "HMOs get high marks from their members," *American Demographics,* February 1994, p. 17.

Braverman, Jordan. *The consumer's book of health: How to stretch your healthcare dollar.* Philadelphia: The Saunders Press, 1982.

Brink S, Newman R. "Living with health reform: Families in four top-flight managed care plans give their views," *U.S. News & World Report,* vol. 115, no. 12, September 27, 1993, p. 38.

Brook R, et al. "Geographic variations in the use of services: Do they have any clinical significance," *Health Affairs,* Summer 1984, p. 63.

Bucci M. "Health maintenance organizations: Plan offerings and enrollments," *Monthly Labor Review,* vol. 114, no. 4, April 1991, pp. 11–19.

Burns J. "Market opening up to non-traditional," *Modern Healthcare,* August 9, 1993, pp. 96–98.

Burr D. "Nurse practitioners . . . cost effective personalized health for women," *Los Angeles Business Journal Supplement,* January 24, 1994, p. 9.

Campion EW. "Why unconventional medicine?" *The New England Journal of Medicine,* January 28, 1993, pp. 282–283.

Clancy CM, Hillner BE. "Physicians as gatekeepers: The impact of financial incentives," *Archives of Internal Medicine,* vol. 149, 1989, pp. 917–920.

Cochrane JD, Miller JL, Pogue JF, eds. "The dynamics of market reform," *Integrated Healthcare Report,* Lake Arrowhead, CA, April 1994, pp. 1–13.

Cochrane JD, Miller JL, Pogue JF, eds. "East meets West," *Integrated Healthcare Report,* Lake Arrowhead, CA, April 1994, pp. 1–13.

Coffey RJ, et al. "An introduction to critical paths," *Quality Management in Healthcare,* vol. 1, 1992, pp. 45–54.

Cohn V. "Making your health plan work for you," *The Washington Post,* November 28, 1989.

Coile RC. "Health care 1992: Top 10 trends for the health field," *Hospital Strategy Report,* vol. 4, no. 3, January 1992, pp. 1–8.

Coile RC. "California hospitals in the 21st century," *California Hospitals,* vol. 7, no. 6, November/December 1993, pp. 6–9.

Coile RC. "Transformation of American healthcare in the post-reform era," *Healthcare Executive,* vol. 9, no. 4, July/August 1994, pp. 8–12.

Dean M. "The gatekeeper: An often overlooked part of reform," *AAPPO Journal,* vol. 3, no. 2, April/May 1993, p. 17–21.

Di Matteo MR, DiNicola DD. *Achieving patient compliance: The psychology of the medical practioner's role.* New York: Pergamon Press, 1982.

Eddy DM. "The anatomy of a decision," *Journal of the American Medical Association,* vol. 263, 1990, pp. 441–443.

Eddy DM. "Practice policies: Guidelines for methods," *Journal of the American Medical Association,* vol. 263, 1990, pp. 1839–1841.

Eddy DM. "Designing a practice policy: Standards, guidelines, and options," *Journal of the American Medical Association,* vol. 263, 1990, pp. 3077–3084.

Eisenberg DM, Kessler RC, Foster C, Norlock FE, Calkins DR, Delbanco TL. "Unconventional medicine in the United States: Prevalence, costs, and patterns of use," *The New England Journal of Medicine,* January 28, 1993, pp. 246–252.

Field MJ, Lohr KN, eds. *Clinical practice guidelines: Directions for a new program.* Washington, DC: National Academy Press, 1990.

Findlay S. "Coverage denied: Your treatment was expensive," *U.S. News & World Report,* vol. 111, no. 24, December 9, 1991, pp. 80–83.

Fishman NT. "The need for ambulatory medical necessity review in multispecialty groups," *Medical Group Management Journal,* July/August 1993, pp. 38–47.

"Five ways to cover the gaps in Medicare," *Consumer Reports,* vol. 59, no. 9, September 1994, p. 574.

Flaherty RJ. "Virtual medical center set up on computer network," *American Medical News,* January 17, 1994, pp. 39–40.

Franks P, Clancy CM, Nutting PA. "Gatekeeping revisited — Protecting patients from overtreatment," *New England Journal of Medicine,* vol. 327, 1992, pp. 427–429.

Gerteis M. "What patients really want," *Health Management Quarterly,* 3rd qtr., 1993, pp. 2–6.

Geyman, J. P. *Family Practice: Foundation of Changing Healthcare,* 2nd ed. Norwalk, CT: Appleton-Century-Crofts, 1985.

Goldman EL. "Provider profiling is not more in-depth, 'valid,' " *Family Practice News,* January 15, 1994, pp. 2, 31.

Gordon S, Shindul-Rothschild J, Woodall P, Watzman N. "The managed care scam: Playing the denial game," *The Nation,* vol. 258, no. 19, May 16, 1994, pp. 657–663.

Gray BB. "2001 hospital odyssey," *LACMA Physician,* Los Angeles Medical Society, Los Angeles, CA, May 2, 1994, pp. 19–25.

Hammonds KH. "The hospital: An inside look at how one institution is struggling to remake itself," *Business Week,* January 17, 1994, pp. 48–61.

Harris and Associates, Louis. *A report card on health maintenance organizations: 1980–1984.* Opinion poll conducted for the Henry J. Kaiser Family Foundation, October 1984.

Health Insurance Association of America. *Managed Care: A health strategy for today and tomorrow.* Washington, DC, 1993.

Henderson N. "Questions to ask before you switch to an HMO," *Kiplinger's Personal Finance Magazine,* vol. 46, no. 5, May 1992, p. 110.

Hofmann PA. "Critical path method: An important tool for coordinating clinical care," *The Joint Commission Journal on Quality Improvement,* vol. 19, no. 7, July 1993, pp. 235–246.

Hood J. "The lessons of TennCare," *National Review,* vol. 46, no. 12, June 27, 1994, pp. 44, 45.

Hornbrook MC, Berki SE. "Practice mode and payment method: Effects on use, costs, quality, and access," *Medical Care,* vol. 23, 1985, pp. 484–511.

Hospital Council of Southern California. "View of the future: 1993–1998," *Center For Health Resources,* Los Angeles, CA, 1992.

Hospital Council of Southern California. "View of the future: 1994–1999," *Center For Health Resources,* Los Angeles, CA, 1993.

"How to buy an HMO," *U.S. News & World Report,* vol. 101, November 10, 1986, p. 60.

Johnson AN, Dowd B, Morris NE, Lurie N. "Differences in inpatient resource use by type of health plan," *Inquiry,* vol. 26, 1989, pp. 388–398.

Joint Commission on the Accreditation of Health Care Organizations, *Accreditation manual for hospitals,* Oakbrook Terrace, IL, 1994.

Kane VL. "Listening to older patients," *Health Management Quarterly,* 3rd qtr., 1993, pp. 11–15.

Kazandjian VA, Lawthers J, Cernak CM, Pipesh FC. "Relating outcomes to processes of care: The Maryland Hospital Association's quality indicator project," *The Joint Commission Journal on Quality Improvement,* November 1993, pp. 530–538.

Kenkel PJ. "Health plans face pressure to find 'report card' criteria that will make the grade," *Modern Healthcare,* January 10, 1994, p. 41.

Kenkel PJ. "Ethix report cared is first for PPOs," *Modern Healthcare,* February 28, 1994, p. 17.

Kenkel PJ. "U.S. Healthcare 'report cards' expanded to primary care docs," *Modern Healthcare,* April 11, 1994, p. 58.

Kenkel PJ. "Alliances for HMO growth," *Modern Healthcare,* vol. 24, no. 18, May 2, 1994, pp. 51–64.

Kongstvedt PR. *The managed healthcare handbook,* 2nd ed. Gaithersburg, MD: Aspen Publishers, Inc., 1993.

Korenjak MF, et al., eds. "Medicaid patients benefit from specialized MCO plans," *CCH Monitor: The Newsletter of Managed Care,* vol. 2, no. 3, February 11, 1994, p. 12.

Kritz FL, Popkin J, Moore LJ. "Health plan choices," *U.S. News & World Report,* vol. 109, no. 3, December 10, 1990, p. 79.

Kuttner R, "Sick joke: The failings of managed care," *The New Republic,* vol. 205, no. 3, December 2, 1991, pp. 20–23.

Lake DB. "Point-of-service plans — the risks and rewards," *Medical Group Management Journal,* July/August 1993, pp. 36–37.

Langan ME. "Do patients have duties?" *Life In Medicine,* June 1993, pp. 6, 7.

Lashley M. "The hidden benefits of case management," *The Employer's Guide to Managed Care,* Managed Care Communications, Inc., Scituate, MA, 1993, pp. 58–59.

Leape LL, Brennan TA, Laird N, et al. "The nature of adverse events in hospitalized patients — results of the Harvard Medical Practice Study II," *New England Journal of Medicine,* vol. 324, 1991, pp. 377–384.

Lewis AB. "Helpful hints in the selection of a utilization review company," *AAPPO Journal,* August/September 1993, pp. 15–21.

Luciano L. "How to size up a doctor network," *Money,* vol. 22, no. 7, July 1993, p. 110.

Malamud P. "Practice parameters may benefit employers," *Business & Health,* June 1992, pp. 34–43.

Manning WG, Leibowitz A, Goldberg GA, Rogers WH, Newhouse JP. "A controlled trial of the effect of a prepaid group practice on use of services," *New England Journal of Medicine,* vol. 310, 1984, pp. 1505–1510.

Marion Merrell Dow managed care digest: HMO edition, 1992. Kansas City, MO: Marion Merrell Dow, Inc., 1992.

Marion Merrell Dow managed care digest: HMO edition, 1993. Kansas City, MO: Marion Merrell Dow, Inc., 1993.

Marion Merrell Dow managed care digest: HMO edition, 1994. Kansas City, MO: Marion Merrell Dow, Inc., 1994.

McGlynn EA. "Gathering systematic information on health plans: An interview with Sheila Leatherman," *The Joint Commision Journal on Quality Improvement,* Joint Commission on the Accreditation of Health Care Organizations, July 1993, pp. 266–272.

"Minnesota's HMO experiment," *Consumer Reports,* vol. 57, no. 9, September 1992, p. 591.

Mettler M, Kemper DW. *Healthwise for life: Medical self-care for healthy aging.* Boise, ID: Healthwise, Inc., 1992.

Miller RH, Luft HS. "Managed care plan performance since 1980," *Journal of the American Medical Association,* vol. 271, no. 19, May 18, 1994, pp. 1512–1519.

Morrissey J. "Maryland project enters 'so-what' phase," *Modern Healthcare,* April 18, 1994, p. 40.

Navarro V. "Wrong medicine," *The Nation,* vol. 256, no. 4, February 1, 1993, p. 113.

Neugebauer JE. "ERISA, Managed care and health reform," *The Monitor,* vol. 22, no. 7, August/September 1993, p. 7.

Noe TJ. "Meaningful measures of health plan quality: Pilot study results from three major employers," *The Employers Guide to Managed Health Care,* Managed Care Communications, Inc., Scituate, MA, 1993, pp. 15–20.

Oberman L. "Grading the report cards," *American Medical News,* February 21, 1994, pp. 3, 44–46.

O'Leary DS. "The measurement mandate: Report card day is coming," *The Joint Commission Journal on Quality Improvement,* November, 1993, pp. 487–491.

Olson R, Gardiner-Jones M, Bezold C. *21st century learning and health care in the home: Creating a national telecommunications network.* Institute of Alternative Futures (Alexandria, VA) and Consumer Interest Research Institute (Washington, DC), January 1992.

Owens DK, Nease RF. "Development of outcome-based practice guidelines: A method for structuring problems and synthesizing evidence," *Journal of Quality Improvement,* vol. 19, no. 7, July 1993, pp. 248–263.

Permut R. "Medical director: An evolving and expanding role of the physician-executive," *Group Practice Journal,* January/February 1989, p. 52.

Pile D. "Measuring quality-guideline management in managed care," *California Physician,* May/June 1994, pp. 7–10.

Poldolsky D, Rubin R, Brink S. "Heal thyself," *U.S. News & World Report,* November 22, 1993, pp. 64–78.

Press I, Malone MP. "Patient satisfaction and the cost/quality equation," *Journal of Health Care Benefits,* November/December 1993, p. 40–43.

Relman AS. "Medical insurance and health: What about managed care?" *The New England Journal of Medicine,* vol. 331, no. 7, August 18, 1994, pp. 471–472.

Richmond S. "Medicare and the HMO switcheroo," *Changing Times,* vol. 44, no. 12, December 1990, p. 93.

Sachs M. "As HMOs know, the key is customer satisfaction," *Modern Healthcare,* June 13, 1994, p. 36.

Simon R. "A flawed remedy: Managed care," *Money,* vol. 22, no. 4, April 1993, p. 114.

Simons A, Hasselbring B, Castleman M. *Before you call the doctor.* New York: Fawcett Columbine, 1992.

Sox HC. "Preventive health services in adults," *The New England Journal of Medicine,* June 2, 1994, pp. 1589–1595.

Spath P. "Choose quality indicators wisely in preparing for your report card," *Hospital Peer Review Newsletter,* September 1994, p. 144–148.

Spencer PL. "More patients being denied health care," *Consumers' Research Magazine,* vol. 76, no. 1, January 1993, p. 25.

Stephenson BJ, Rowe BH, Haynes RB, Macharia WM, Leon G. "Is the patient taking the treatment prescribed?" *Journal of the American Medical Association,* vol. 269, no. 21, June 2, 1993, pp. 2779–2781.

Stevens L. "Ain't misbehavin'," *American Medical News,* February 21, 1994.

Stewart JM. *American values and health care reform, 1993.* Albany, NY: Novalis National Health Care Survey, Novalis Corporation, March 1993.

Stewart JM. *Consumer ratings of managed care: A special report, 1993.* Albany, NY: Novalis National Health Care Survey, Novalis Corporation, October 1993.

Vogel S, Manhoff D. *Emergency medical treatment.* Wilmette, IL: EMT, Inc. Publishing, 1989.

Wennberg JE. "The paradox of appropriate care," *Journal of the American Medical Association,* vol. 258, 1987, pp. 2568–2569.

Wilcox MD. "Getting your share from managed care," *Kiplinger's Personal Finance Magazine,* vol. 47, no. 2, February 1993, p. 63.

Williams G. "Does it pay to join an HMO?" *Woman's Day,* vol. 52, no. 10, June 10, 1989, p. 32.

Winslow R. "In health care, low cost beats high quality," *The Wall Street Journal,* January 1, 1994, p. B1.

Winslow R. "An HMO tries talking members into healthy habits," *The Wall Street Journal*, April 6, 1994.

Winslow R. "Health care report cards are getting low grades," *The Wall Street Journal*, May 19, 1994.

Wolfe S, ed. "How you can make HMOs more accountable," *Health Letter,* Public Citizen Health Research Group, Washington, DC, November 1991, pp. 1–4.

Wood SD. "Getting to the bottom line in health plans," *Group Practice Journal,* January/February 1989, pp. 49–51.

Zane M. "Health care 2007," *Business—Diagnosis; Supplement to the Los Angeles Business Journal,* June 27, 1994, pp. 32–34.

Index

Body temperature, severity of illness and, 84
Breast cancer screening, 74

Cancer screening, 73, 74
Capitation, 158
Cardiopulmonary resuscitation (CPR) in living will, 138
Care maps, 85–86
Case management, 97–102
  action plans and, 100
  assessment and, 99–100
  authorization of services and, 79
  for chronic diseases, 74
  eligibility for, 97–98
  implementing plans for, 100
  monitoring progress and, 100–101
  programs for, 13
  reasons for use of, 98–99
  results of, 101–102
  screening and, 99
Case managers
  as managed care team members, 10
  relationship with, 101
Cervical cancer screening, 73
Chemical dependency, rehabilitation programs for, 74
Choice of providers
  choosing an HMO and, 43
  limitations on, 13
  under POS plans, 22
Cholesterol screening, 74
Choosing a provider, 57–60
Choosing an HMO, 41–48
  access to care and, 44–45
  benefit plans and, 43–44
  convenience and, 14, 45
  cost and, 42–43
  degree of choice and, 43
  organizational structure and, 45–46
  quality and, 47–48
  reputation and, 42
  responsiveness to members and, 48
  summary decision sheet for, 54–55
  utilization management and, 47

Chronic diseases, case management for, 74
CIGNA Health Plan, 17
Claims processing department, 46
Clinical laboratory, hospital accreditation and, 163
Collaboration of patient and physician, 118–120
Colon cancer screening, 74
Communication system, future of, 171–173
Community involvement of hospitals, 64
Competency, continuing care planning and, 111
Competitive market, costs and, 158
Complaints. *See* Problem prevention and resolution
Computer reports, 94
Computers in medical education, 176
Concurrent review, 92
Consumers. *See* Patient(s)
Continuing care planners as managed care team members, 10
Continuing care planning, 93–94, 109–115
  benefits of, 109–110
  checklist for, 112
  family involvement in, 111–112
  functions of, 110–111
  long-term care and, 115
  premature discharge and, 112–114
  problems in, 114–115
Contracted providers, authorization of services and, 78
Contracting
  policies for, 93
  selective, 158
Convenience, choosing an HMO and, 14, 45
Coordination of care, 12–13
  under Medicare, 35
Copayments, 155–156, 158
  under Medicare, 34
  under POS plans, 22